The World of
Velázquez

TIME-LIFE LIBRARY OF ART

The World of Velázquez

1599 - 1660

by Dale Brown
and
the Editors of TIME-LIFE BOOKS

TIME-LIFE BOOKS, New York

TIME-LIFE BOOKS

FOUNDER: Henry R. Luce 1898-1967

Editor-in-Chief: Hedley Donovan
Chairman of the Board: Andrew Heiskell
President: James R. Shepley
Group Vice President: Rhett Austell

Vice Chairman: Roy E. Larsen

MANAGING EDITOR: Jerry Korn
Assistant Managing Editors: Ezra Bowen,
David Maness, Martin Mann, A. B. C. Whipple
Planning Director: Oliver E. Allen
Art Director: Sheldon Cotler
Chief of Research: Beatrice T. Dobie
Director of Photography: Melvin L. Scott
Senior Text Editor: Diana Hirsh
Assistant Art Director: Arnold C. Holeywell
Assistant Chief of Research: Myra Mangan

PUBLISHER: Joan D. Manley
General Manager: John D. McSweeney
Business Manager: Nicholas J. C. Ingleton
Sales Director: Carl G. Jaeger
Promotion Director: Paul R. Stewart
Public Relations Director: Nicholas Benton

TIME-LIFE LIBRARY OF ART
SERIES EDITOR: Robert Morton
Associate Editor: Diana Hirsh
Editorial Staff for *The World of Velázquez:*
Text Editor: Jay Brennan
Designer: Paul Jensen
Staff Writers: John von Hartz, David Lawton,
Paula Pierce, Lucille Schulberg
Chief Researcher: Martha T. Goolrick
Researchers: Jill N. Beasley, Villette Harris,
Jane Peterson, Susanna Seymour
Art Assistant: Mervyn Clay

EDITORIAL PRODUCTION
Production Editor: Douglas B. Graham
Assistant Production Editors: Gennaro C. Esposito,
Feliciano Madrid
Quality Director: Robert L. Young
Assistant Quality Director: James J. Cox
Copy Staff: Rosalind Stubenberg (chief),
Patricia Miller, Florence Keith, Pearl Sverdlin
Picture Department: Dolores A. Littles, Catherine Ireys

About the Author

Dale Brown is Assistant International Editor for TIME-LIFE BOOKS. He is the author of three volumes in the FOODS OF THE WORLD series, *The Cooking of Scandinavia, American Cooking* and *American Cooking: The Northwest.* He also wrote the picture essays in three other books in this series, *Michelangelo, Vermeer* and *Winslow Homer.*

The Consulting Editor

H. W. Janson is Professor of Fine Arts at New York University, where he is also Chairman of the Department of Fine Arts at Washington Square College. Among his many publications are *History of Art* and *The Sculpture of Donatello.*

The Consultant for This Book

Priscilla E. Muller, Curator of Paintings at the Hispanic Society of America in New York City, has taught baroque art at Brooklyn College and has lectured at numerous institutions. She is the author of many articles and reviews on Spanish art. Dr. Muller is a Corresponding Member of the Real Academia de Ciencias, Bellas Letras y Nobles Artes de Córdoba and the Hispanic Society of America.

On the Slipcase

This detail from Velázquez' *Las Meninas (page 178)* portrays the Princess Margarita, daughter of Philip IV and his Queen, Mariana of Austria.

End Papers

These watercolor views of Madrid were executed in the late 17th Century by Pier Maria Baldi, an Italian artist. The scene in the front of the book shows the Alcázar, where Velázquez lived and worked. Biblioteca Medicea-Laurenziana, Florence.

The following individuals and departments of Time Inc. helped to produce this book: Editorial Production, Norman Airey; Library, Benjamin Lightman; Picture Collection, Doris O'Neil; Photographic Laboratory, George Karas; TIME-LIFE News Service, Murray J. Gart; Correspondents Maria Vincenza Aloisi (Paris), Jean Bratton (Madrid), Friso Endt (Amsterdam), Margot Hapgood (London), Martha Haymaker (Beverly Hills), Dick Hitt (Dallas), Elisabeth Kraemer (Bonn), Traudl Lessing (Vienna), Knud Meister (Copenhagen), Ann Natanson (Rome) and Gavin Scott (Boston).

Contents

I

The Lure
of Madrid

Half in shadow, Diego de Silva Velázquez, the greatest of Spanish painters, looks out at us from the greatest of his paintings, *Las Meninas,* or *The Ladies in Waiting.* This is no self-portrait in the great tradition of a Rembrandt, who so often bared his soul for all to see. It is merely Velázquez' statement of how he happened to appear in a certain light *(detail, left)* on an afternoon in 1656. He then stood at the peak of his career, dignified by fame, honored by Spain's proud and apparently all-powerful King—and yet he saw fit to show himself only as a part of the whole, as nothing more than an element in an overall composition *(page 178).* Search the shadowed face for some clue to his personality and you come up with questions instead of answers. Is that melancholy in those black eyes, or is it reserve?

For one so famous in his own lifetime, a painter of kings and queens, it is curious that so little should be known about Velázquez the man. References to him by his contemporaries are few and contradictory. An Englishman who knew him only slightly called him lazy. An Italian passed on the obvious canard that he never finished his paintings. Another found him "clever in his speech." The King wrote of his "well-known phlegm." A poet described him as a person who breathed dignity. His father-in-law and teacher, the artist Francisco Pacheco, saw him as a genius. An 18th Century biographer, drawing upon firsthand witnesses for his own brief account of Velázquez' life, praised his "fine, natural disposition."

To uncover the real Velázquez, we must turn to his art—and to his troubled times. If he stands in shadow, his world does not, and the people he portrayed were movers and shakers in that world. In his depicting of them, we see his world, and in turn we see him. No matter how unassuming the artist may have been, we feel his presence everywhere in his paintings, and the longer we look at them, the more he seems to speak to us from them, quietly and serenely. Thus, indirectly, he tells us a great deal about himself.

I first came under his spell in Madrid's great museum, the Prado—in the large back room where *Las Meninas* hangs in majestic isolation. Here the dim light almost exactly duplicates the light in the painting, a green-

His face seen only dimly, Diego Velázquez has the look of a man who all his life concerned himself with seeking and revealing truth. He painted this self-portrait after more than three decades of loyal service to Philip IV, at a time when Spain stood close to ruin.

Detail from *Las Meninas*

ish light, and the walls of the room are a soft gray like those in Velázquez' studio. You are invited, in this setting, to enter the world of the painting, and you do so, automatically. It is a quiet world, in which a king and queen seem to pose for their portrait. But what a strange portrait Velázquez has given us: the royal pair is seen as a reflection in a distant mirror, while a glowing little girl, who is to the tip of her toes a princess, and an assortment of lesser characters, including two dwarfs, fill the foreground. A hush has fallen over the room. A dog, wreathed by rolls and wrinkles of fur and flesh, slumbers contentedly to the right. Only the boy dwarf threatens to disturb the stillness by nudging the animal with his foot. The Princess looks intently ahead. One of her ladies in waiting is at the lowest dip of a curtsey. Another has just risen. The artist has stepped back from his canvas. All motion seems to have stopped, and with it, time.

Look again at *Las Meninas* in its thick ebony frame and you can understand why the critic Théophile Gautier, seeing it for the first time, asked, "Where is the painting?" It appears to have been done so effortlessly you hardly notice how much effort went into it. To analyze its beauties is almost to defile them and yet, caught up in their magic, you find you must. You think the painting consists of many colors until you look again and realize that it contains few; it is a harmony of browns, grays, reds and greens. And miraculously, the illusion of depth, so strong in *Las Meninas,* is achieved not solely by lines of perspective reaching back into the canvas, but by paint, subtle gradations of paint that capture light in the very act of hollowing out space. You are suddenly aware that Velázquez could accomplish anything he set his mind and brushes to. Moreover, you also recognize that he was so secure as a painter, so in command of his talent, that he had no need to show off his skills. He could afford to be self-effacing.

Another way to know Velázquez is to explore the setting that *Las Meninas* represents, the court of Philip IV from 1621 to 1665. As painter to the King, Velázquez worked and eventually came to live in the royal palace, and his paintings are the mirror of that environment and of the people who filled it. He served Philip loyally through four decades, through the decline and near-fall of Spain that drove King and nobles into a world of dreams and unreality. Madrid went mad as Spain fell apart, and Velázquez was witness to it all. Knowing, as I now do, a good deal about the times in which he lived, I find myself more amazed today by *Las Meninas* than when I first stood in front of it and succumbed to it. For the question in my mind no longer is how did he do it, but how could Velázquez have painted at all?

At the outset of the painter's career, Velázquez and Spain had reason to be optimistic. The country had a new king, and a young one. Philip IV was only 16 when he came to power in 1621. His youth, far from being viewed as a handicap, was regarded by his subjects as a reason for hope, the first real hope they had allowed themselves in years. After the disastrous reign of his father, Philip III, during which Spain had come to the very edge of ruin, they thought that it might just be possible that a boy, wisely advised and starting out fresh, could save the country and bring back its glory. In reality, it was a task for a titan: the economy was in such bad shape that future revenues had been pledged to pay off outstanding loans; the currency was debased and inflation was rampant; foreign and domestic affairs were in complete disorder; the court was riddled with corruption; and the once-powerful Spanish Navy now consisted of seven warships. Worse, considered from the point of view of the national welfare, the Crown stood committed to the defense of the forces of Roman Catholicism against the new faith of Protestantism. Little did anyone dream that the aid now being extended by Spain to her Austrian ally, the Holy Roman Emperor Ferdinand II, on behalf of the Catholic cause signaled great sacrifice for Spain. The small war then being fought by the Emperor in Bohemia over the religious issue was the beginning of one of the most protracted wars in history, the Thirty Years' War, one which was to empty Spain's treasury, dishearten her king and his ministers and, in the end, leave proud Spain revealed as a hollow giant, a bad last in the struggle for European hegemony.

But all this lay ahead. As a young painter, Velázquez had more reason than most to feel confident about the future. He had been a brilliant pupil in the studio of Francisco Pacheco, and his master had been much impressed by his talent; indeed, Pacheco had given him his only daughter in marriage in 1618. He had established a solid reputation for himself as a painter of the first rank in his native Seville. He had had, in fact, the altogether rare experience for a young artist of finding himself an influence on others almost as soon as he acquired the credentials of a master from the Seville painters' guild. What had brought him his first recognition —and set others to copying him—were his paintings of plain people and simple objects, in which he seemed to penetrate to the heart of matter. He promised to bring something original to Spanish art.

But successful and happy as Velázquez may have been in Seville, he apparently had other ideas in mind. If he remained there, he could be certain of having as his patron the Church, which had already granted him a number of commissions. But his bent was clearly for the secular rather than the spiritual. There was only one place for an artist of his talent and inclination to work, and that was the Madrid court.

Thus, in the spring of 1622, Velázquez set out for the capital. His purpose ostensibly was to see the famous collection of European paintings housed in the Escorial, the monastery-palace some 30 miles from the city, but he also went in the undisguised hope of painting portraits of his youthful sovereigns, Philip and his queen, Isabel. As it turned out, the King was too busy to pose for him. But Velázquez was at least spared the indignity of having to display his work on the Calle Mayor, Madrid's busiest street, in the hope thereby of capturing some important person's eye. This was the procedure followed by other aspiring artists. At Pacheco's behest, Velázquez painted one of the leading intellectuals at court, the poet Don Luis de Góngora. The picture is a stark and forceful analysis of a hawkish man of strong character, with a deeply lined face and intense eyes, so black that the pupils cannot easily be made out in them. Pacheco wrote in *The Art of Painting*, the book which contains most of the basic information about Velázquez, that the portrait was

CHARLES V
Holy Roman Emperor 1519-1556
King of Spain 1516-1556

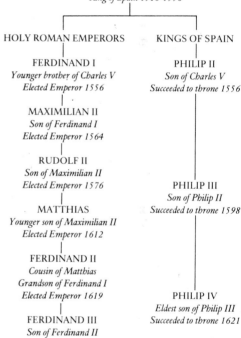

HOLY ROMAN EMPERORS

FERDINAND I
Younger brother of Charles V
Elected Emperor 1556

MAXIMILIAN II
Son of Ferdinand I
Elected Emperor 1564

RUDOLF II
Son of Maximilian II
Elected Emperor 1576

MATTHIAS
Younger son of Maximilian II
Elected Emperor 1612

FERDINAND II
Cousin of Matthias
Grandson of Ferdinand I
Elected Emperor 1619

FERDINAND III
Son of Ferdinand II
Elected Emperor 1637

KINGS OF SPAIN

PHILIP II
Son of Charles V
Succeeded to throne 1556

PHILIP III
Son of Philip II
Succeeded to throne 1598

PHILIP IV
Eldest son of Philip III
Succeeded to throne 1621

The long alliance between Spain and the Holy Roman Empire began when both crowns rested on one head—that of Charles V, whose coat of arms is above. In 1556 Charles abdicated his powers, consigning the Imperial title to his brother and the Spanish crown to his son, so that both realms remained under Habsburg domination. By Velázquez' time, a century later, King Philip IV of Spain, great-grandson of Charles V, found himself, because of successive intermarriages, related to the Holy Roman Emperor, Ferdinand III, as cousin, brother-in-law and son-in-law.

Spain in the time of Philip IV was not a unified nation, but rather the fragmented federation of semi-independent kingdoms and provinces shown on this map. Philip held rights over three large areas called "crowns": Portugal, Castile and Aragon. Castile, Spain's large, central region, was itself divided into 10 territories including the autonomous Basque Provinces. It was the richest of Philip's three crowns, for New World treasure flowed through its ports. But Castile was heavily taxed to support Philip's court at Madrid. Aragon incorporated the kingdom of Aragon as well as Catalonia and fertile Valencia. Portugal commanded a huge stretch of Atlantic coastline. Each crown had its own Cortes, or parliament, and a proud sense of its identity.

"very celebrated in Madrid." And thus before going home, the 23-year-old artist gave the capital good reason to remember his name.

The way to the King, however, was not to be through Góngora, but through His Majesty's right-hand man, Don Gaspar de Guzmán, Count of Olivares and Duke of San Lúcar. Here Velázquez was again fortunate. Olivares was not only a connoisseur of the arts, but a Sevillian like himself. Pacheco had painted the Minister's portrait as early as 1610, and Olivares had undoubtedly come often to Pacheco's studio, which was a gathering place for the aristocrats and intellectuals of Seville. Even if Velázquez himself had not met Olivares, he could count among his Sevillian admirers several who now were closely associated with Olivares at the court. One of the witnesses at the artist's wedding had been Francisco de Rioja, a poet and friend of Olivares.

After Velázquez had returned home, his admirers in Madrid applied themselves to the task of winning for him the all-important patronage of Olivares—who in October of 1622 rose to the most prestigious post in the realm, that of First Minister. Luck was on Velázquez' side; the King's favorite court painter had died, and in the spring came Olivares' summons. Once again Velázquez set out for Madrid, this time with Pacheco, who smelled success in the air and wanted to share in the glory.

And indeed there promised to be all sorts of glory for anyone connected with the new monarchy. Great change was anticipated for Spain. Nothing would do but that she again become a first-rate power. The potential certainly was there. Despite her internal exhaustion, she ruled over the Kingdoms of Sicily and Naples, the Duchy of Milan, and the part of the Netherlands called Flanders *(map, page 26)*; overseas she held vast territories in the Americas and in the Far East. Spanish troops fighting in Germany on behalf of the Austrian Emperor and in Flanders against heretical Dutchmen were doing well. All this was read as a sign that the old aggressive spirit that had led to the conquest of the New

World and planted the Spanish flag in the Philippines was yet alive.

Even more important, it looked as though the mess at home could be straightened out. Olivares was working on a bold new plan to unify Spain. The España of his day consisted of several separately governed states—Castile, the seat of the monarchy, Portugal, Aragon, Valencia and Catalonia *(map, page 10)*. Even though Castile ostensibly stood at the head of these, with Philip the king of all, it could expect little help from them. Each paid a small tribute to the Crown, but each took responsibility for its own defense. Allegiance stopped where Castile's involvement in European affairs began. Olivares, who understood only too well that "kings cannot achieve heroic actions without money," recognized the need to bring the other states into closer cooperation with Castile. His idea was to establish a mutual defense organization, the so-called Union of Arms, that would oblige the Spaniards to think and act collectively. Each state would contribute men as well as money to the overall cause of Spanish arms and each would come to the aid of the others in case of attack. Olivares saw this sharing of responsibility not only as a way of building a new and more powerful army and navy, but of reducing the heavy tax load that formerly had fallen on Castile alone.

Behind Olivares' plan for the Union of Arms lay a much more ambitious scheme, and this he revealed to the King in a secret memorandum: "Let your Majesty hold as the most important affair of your State to make yourself *King of Spain*. I mean, Sire, that you should not content yourself with being King of Portugal, of Aragon, of Valencia, Count of Barcelona, but that you should secretly plan and work to reduce these realms of which Spain consists to the laws and forms of Castile, without any distinction. If your Majesty succeeds in this, you will be the most powerful prince in the world."

To lay the groundwork for the Union of Arms, Olivares and the young King first turned their attentions to Castile, and launched a series of reforms. Appropriately, the royal household was the first to feel the sweep of the broom. Shortly before Velázquez' arrival in Madrid the royal staff had been reduced, salaries cut and rations curtailed. The economies effected were at times petty—the chief stewards were no longer to receive free dishes of chicken or rice, nor daily allowances of ice—but the King himself estimated that the savings would come to 67,000 ducats (the annual cost of maintaining troops in Flanders was more than 3.5 million ducats). To set an example, Philip took to wearing modest garb and gave few feasts. "So I have reconciled myself to ask for nothing for my own person," he wrote, "but only the indispensable funds for the defense of my realm and the Catholic faith. I want no more."

In more sweeping measures, royal grants and pensions were cut back and an attempt was made to slash the number of municipal offices by two thirds. Brothels were closed and laws passed against ostentation. The rich were to limit the number of their servants, restrict their use of coaches, and, among other things, imitate their king by avoiding finery, including the white ruffs with which they so proudly set off their faces.

The last prohibition had its foolish overtones. A whole storm brewed over it—and the recovery of the national economy was made to seem dependent on its enforcement. "A single ruff of linen with its making and ravelling will cost over 200 reals, and six reals every time it is dressed," argued one of the reformers in a memorandum to the King. "Besides, many strong, able young men are employed in dressing and goffering [starching and fluting] these extravagant things, who might be better employed in work necessary for the commonwealth or in tilling the ground. The servants, too, have to be paid higher wages in consequence of the money they spend in wearing these collars, which indeed consumes most of what they earn; and a great quantity of wheat, which is sorely wanted for food, is wasted in starch. The fine linens to make these collars have, moreover, to be brought from abroad, and money has to be sent out of the country to pay for them."

Punishment for anyone caught wearing the ruff became the pillory and banishment. But what to wear instead? The only neckcloth acceptable to the reformers, the so-called Walloon collar, hung like an unstarched table napkin on the shoulders and soiled easily. Before long, however, a Madrid tailor came up with an alternative: the *golilla,* a wide-flaring collar. It was made of cardboard and covered with white or gray silk on top and dark cloth underneath, and its advantage over the Walloon collar was that it remained stiff without starching and could be worn as long as a year without being washed. But the issue was not easily resolved: the tailor ran afoul of the Inquisition for his invention. Surely, the ubiquitous investigators reasoned, a man poking around at the back of a shop with cardboard, rollers to bend the cardboard and steaming pots of shellac with which to stiffen it must be up to witchcraft of some kind. The hapless tailor was called before the Holy Office and might have been imprisoned had not Olivares intervened. The King had seen the *golilla* and liked it; in fact, he had ordered several, but they had been burned in the street by zealots unaware that the condemned collars were intended for His Majesty. Olivares was furious, the tailor was released, the King got his collars, and the *golilla* caught on. It is so conspicuous an article of dress in most of the portraits by Velázquez that the *golilla* today seems the emblem of Philip's reign.

Velázquez—himself no doubt quick to adopt the *golilla*—was to be very much a part of the new order. After arriving a second time in the capital, he settled in the home of Don Juan de Fonseca, a fellow Sevillian and one of the King's chaplains, and began there a portrait of his host. As soon as it was finished, the painting, now lost, was carried to the Alcázar, the gloomy royal residence on the bluff above the Manzanares River, and within the hour it had been praised by everybody, from the courtiers to the King's two brothers to Philip himself. As a result, Velázquez was given a commission to paint the younger of the princes, Fernando. But, as Pacheco reveals with modest pride in his book, "it was thought more appropriate" that Velázquez should first execute a portrait of the King.

Although the portrait of Fonseca, like the earlier one of Góngora, had been greatly admired, and the artist's name was now known throughout the palace, the King again could not spare the time to pose for Velázquez. The Prince of Wales, the future Charles I of England, had come without advance notice to Madrid, under the most surprising circum-

Velázquez' first portrait of Philip IV *(above)* was a realistic view of the 19-year-old King that accurately reflected his less than prepossessing appearance. Over this likeness the artist sometime later painted a new portrait so that the original can today be seen only by X-ray.

This is the refinement Velázquez painted over the first portrait. The artist was now concerned more with portraying Philip the King than Philip the man. The pose is basically the same, but the shoulders are thrown back, the hands are more graceful, and the legs are in balance.

stances. He had ridden horseback across France and Spain in 16 days in the company of only three men. His object was to woo Philip's blond and full-lipped sister María, and to carry her off to England with him as his bride. In this harebrained journey he had the full blessing of his father, James I, who saw the marriage serving a double purpose. One was purely practical: María's dowry would be a boon to England. The second was of a face-saving nature: James had long been disturbed by the fact that his son-in-law Frederick, the Elector Palatine and husband of his favorite daughter, had lost the Rhenish Palatinate at the outset of the Thirty Years' War. His son-in-law's state along the Rhine was now in

As the detail from Velázquez' first painting of Philip *(preceding page)* shows, the King was in fact a rather ugly man. But Spanish taste ran to realism, and the work was a popular success until Velázquez painted it out of sight.

This more idealized view of Philip was painted after Velázquez had been at the royal court a year. In this third portrait, the artist lengthened the King's neck, narrowed his face, sharpened his chin, and gave him a cleft above Cupid's-bow lips—making him a handsome young ruler indeed.

the possession of Spain and her Austrian ally, and James hoped to retrieve it for Frederick and his wife.

At first Philip and Olivares were at a loss: a good Catholic like María could never be allowed to marry a heretic like the Protestant Charles. Then Olivares saw a way to turn the situation to Spain's advantage. They would pretend to be in favor of the marriage in order to extract as many concessions and promises from Charles and his father as possible. And with this end in mind, they spared nothing to make the Prince's stay a long and splendid one. The King and Olivares were even willing to suspend the laws against the wearing of finery that they had so recently ini-

In 1626, after three years at court, Velázquez not only further refined Philip's features in still another portrait of the King, but gave him a luminous, pearl-like complexion with the inner glow of saintliness.

The so-called *Brown and Silver Philip,* from which this detail is taken, shows another step in the evolution of Velázquez' conception of Philip. Painted in 1632, the face is free of lines, the hair is touched by golden light, the eyebrow is arched knowingly. It is not just a portrait of a man, but a vision of a king.

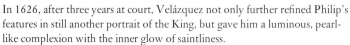

tiated, and like a desert after a rainstorm, the capital burst into bloom.

Madrid was not a lovely city, and it welcomed any opportunity to dress up and hide its drab face. Now it had brilliant reason to do so. Not much more than a village before the government moved there in 1561, the city had grown haphazardly, overflowing its boundaries and spreading out, as Góngora said, like the Nile. The majority of its dun-colored houses were one-story affairs of no architectural distinction whatever. Yet people flocked to Madrid from all over the country to be near the court, "the last phosphorescent spot in a decaying body," as the historian Martin Hume so eloquently put it. They had made it a center of high living

Painted in 1624, not long after Velázquez had arrived at court, this portrait of the Count of Olivares, the formidable figure who was Philip IV's First Minister, conveys an impression of power. The shoulders set off the strong face; the trappings of office adorn the Minister's torso.

So bluntly rendered was Velázquez' first portrait of Olivares that scholars long quarreled over its authenticity. This second study shows a more subtle Velázquez at work. The Minister remains impressive but, as in the successive portraits of the King, he has acquired grace.

and fashion, where women flounced about in absurdly wide skirts, and gentlemen wore locks dangling down in front of their ears. With the relaxation of regulations, the old finery reappeared and giddiness replaced sobriety. Processions, bullfights, tourneys, balls and masques followed one after another, all in honor of Charles.

This, then, was the mood of the city in which Velázquez found himself waiting for his chance to paint the King. How he spent his time during these dizzying days is not known, but no doubt he took advantage of the opportunity Olivares' patronage gave him to explore the Alcázar. The royal collection of masterpieces by Titian hung in black frames in vaulted rooms overlooking a courtyard filled with statues and busts. Tapestries, some 800 in all and reputedly the finest in Europe, covered walls throughout the palace. And cramming the corridors were paintings of many different kinds.

The King's paintings were also much admired by Prince Charles, himself an enthusiastic collector, and toward the end of his visit in Spain, he was taken to the Escorial to see the prize canvases hanging there. Velázquez went along on this tour and made a sketch in color of Charles, for which he received 100 escudos.

After he had been in Spain some five months, the Prince made ready to depart, the negotiations between him and Philip having come to nothing. Right to the end the pleasantries kept up. Charles knew that he had been made the fool, but he had no other choice than to put on a good face. A lavish exchange of gifts took place, and the King, though glad to see him go and delighted to have denied him María, donned "a blacke sute, and jewals, for the sorrow of the Prince's departure."

It was in the closing days of Charles's visit that Philip finally found time to sit for Velázquez. For the young artist his subject posed something of a problem. In the past, he had concentrated on portraits of much older men, and between him and his sitters there had always been the respectful distance of age. Now he was confronted by a man six years his junior. If this was not in itself something of a challenge, how must he have felt painting an 18-year-old who happened not only to be his king, but who ruled an empire that extended into Italy and northern Europe and stretched halfway around the globe? He nevertheless managed to paint the portrait in short order—Pacheco says in one day.

Upon seeing the portrait for the first time, Olivares announced publicly that no one had ever really painted the King before Velázquez. The court agreed. Indeed, Philip and Olivares were so impressed by the talent of the young painter from Seville that they arranged in October to take him into the King's employ at a salary of 20 ducats a month. For this he was to execute any paintings that might be demanded of him. Even before the month was out, the agreement was amended very much to the artist's advantage: he would get the 20 ducats, and in addition, he would be paid for each new painting. He was ordered to transfer his household from Seville to Madrid. Moreover, he was told that henceforth he would be the only painter to portray the King, and as proof of this, existing portraits of Philip were to be removed from public view. Velázquez was then 24 years old.

That first royal portrait, the one that opened so many doors for Velázquez, was obviously something special. It tantalized art scholars over the years, for it disappeared from sight in Velázquez' own day. Then in 1960 it turned up in Spain—in the Prado of all places—*under* the surface of another full-length portrait of Philip that had been X-rayed for a study of the artist's methods. What the X-rays revealed was startling.

Our own idea of Philip's appearance has been formed almost entirely by Velázquez' portraits of him, and it is next to impossible to think that he could have looked any different from the way Velázquez painted him over a 40-year period. In all the 10 surviving portraits, Philip has a long, narrow face, with drooping eyelids and a prominent nose. His lower lip thrusts out and his low-slung jaw projects from the stem of a medium-length neck. An odd-looking man, certainly. But in the X-rays revealing that first portrait *(page 13),* Philip showed up looking odder still. His chin is large and blunt, his cheeks are puffy, and his neck is so short that it bulges like a stump from a wide-flaring *golilla.*

How could the discrepancy between this, Velázquez' initial view of Philip, and the portrait he painted over it be explained? Examination of the X-rays revealed that the original painting had been slightly damaged —but retouching it would surely have been a less drastic expedient than covering it completely. Although the overpainted picture was executed perhaps five years after the original, time alone could not account for such marked changes in Philip's physiognomy. Besides, there were two intervening portraits *(pages 14 and 15)* to compare to the "lost" work, and they showed Philip looking himself—that is, as we have been conditioned by Velázquez to think he looked. Only one conclusion could be drawn: that the artist had deliberately set about to modify Philip's features.

Was flattery the reason? Apparently not. Philip had liked the original portrait; neither he nor Olivares nor the court had found the likeness unflattering. What, then, could have been Velázquez' motive?

The answer is tied up in the religious and political beliefs of the day and in the nature of the artist's response to the King; and it tells us something more about Velázquez. After finishing the first royal portrait, he came to know Philip. He must have felt an empathy with a man who, like himself, was young and starting out in life, and who shared his passion for art. Their relationship soon developed beyond the formal one of king and subject, sitter and painter, to one of human dimensions. Philip began visiting Velázquez' studio almost daily to watch him at work. During these relaxed encounters, Velázquez came to appreciate the burdens borne by Philip. Not only was Philip expected to restore Spain's greatness, but to act according to his title, Defender of the Faith. For along with the crown, he had inherited the policy of his predecessors, the defense of Catholicism against the divisive forces of the Protestant heresy. As a Spaniard and a Catholic, Velázquez would sympathize with this view of the quasi-divine nature of the King. He probably needed very little urging, if any at all, from Olivares to project into his portraits of the King what Pablo Picasso has called Philip IV's "right of might."

Through the manipulation of Velázquez' brush, Philip indeed began to look like a monarch who could restore Spain's grandeur and make Catholicism again triumphant in Europe. The artist began by subtly extending the length of Philip's neck and shaping his blunt chin. He also turned the King's sallow complexion to advantage, re-creating it and enhancing it on the canvas with layers of almost transparent glazes that make the skin seem to glow, as though illumined from within by a holy light. And to all this he added his compassion; while Philip may appear a man apart, he is also in Velázquez' portraits a human being.

Despite the steps the artist took to enhance Philip's appearance, he did not flatter his subject. Perhaps more amazing, considering the critical audience in the court, he did not attempt to catch the eye with meticulously rendered detail or ostentatious demonstrations of skill with the brush; even that first portrait, from which Velázquez had so much to gain, is distinguished by its restraint. What the paintings possess is dignity, a dignity that obviously was not just Philip's, but Velázquez' as well, the mark of all his work. By refusing to pander, he shows us how much he remained his own man, incapable of painting anything that he himself did not believe in.

Look closely at the portrait of Philip that now covers Velázquez' first effort (*page 13*), and see how masterful it is in its simplicity. The King stands in a gray-green space, with light and shadow creating a sense of depth. Philip's pale face is smoothed and molded by light, as are his left hand, resting on the table, and his right, holding a petition. The harmonious play of blacks and grays throughout, punctuated softly by the deep smoldering red of a tablecloth, lends enormous strength to the subject. Shown without any of the panoply of power, Philip is nevertheless every inch the king.

Such understatement is yet another mark of Velázquez' art. He eliminated all that he considered extraneous, and in doing so he let his subject matter speak for itself, let its inner worth shine through.

It is strange that after having painted the King so well, Velázquez should have gone so far off the mark in his first portrait of his patron, Olivares (*page 16*). Here, dressed in a puffy black suit and encumbered by the insignia of his high office, including a chain, spurs and an outsized key, the Minister looms like a genie sprung from a bottle. Perhaps Velázquez owed him too large a debt to have approached the commission with ease, or perhaps he was intimidated by Olivares' brusqueness, which had already won the Minister many enemies in the court. There are people today who are so much put off by this painting that they refuse to accept it as a Velázquez, and more than one critic has noted that the head is disproportionately small for the massive body.

A second portrait of Olivares (*page 16*), done a year later, in 1625, is far more successful, a distillation of the Minister's personality and manner. Painting him well could not have been an easy chore, especially if reality was to be served: Olivares was portly and chunky, and had rounded shoulders and a bulbous, rubbery-looking nose. On top of his squarish head he wore a black, shaggy wig—which he would occasionally prop up with a stick, presumably to let the air in. In this second portrait of Olivares, Velázquez managed both to capture the brutal force of the man and to supply him with a certain dash appropriate to his long list of titles. He showed Olivares, an excellent horseman, holding bolt upright in his right hand a riding whip, as appropriate a symbol of his power as any.

In a figurative sense at least, Olivares had begun to crack that whip. He pushed aggressively ahead with his plan for the Union of Arms despite opposition from the subordinate states; in 1626 he went with the King to Aragon, Valencia and Catalonia to ask their ruling bodies to provide men and money for the common cause. All along the line he met resistance; his mistake, like that of many another statesman, was to apply too much pressure. The Aragonese and the Valencians bluntly refused to supply men. They did, however, reluctantly part with some money. The

Although Philip IV often paid Velázquez in ducats, a gold coinage that had originated in 1252 in Florence, the common Spanish currencies were based on the escudo, a gold coin, and the real (above), which was made of silver. Reals came in denominations of eight, four, two, one, and one half. When smaller coins were in short supply, larger ones were cut into segments. (The American expression "two bits" for a quarter of a dollar derives from the two one-eighth "bits" of an eight-real coin that made up one quarter of its full value.) Shown is a coin of eight reals, familiar from pirate lingo as a "piece of eight." The obverse of the coin (top) displays the shield of the House of Habsburg with an assayer's mark to the left and the value to the right; on the reverse are the provincial arms of Castile and León.

Catalans stubbornly opposed all of Olivares' demands, and the Minister and the King left in a huff for Madrid.

It is amazing that someone as unassuming and subtle as Velázquez, serving a man like Olivares, should have succeeded so brilliantly in the court. Yet the number of commissions and honors bestowed upon him increased steadily during the early years of his royal service. A large portrait he did of Philip on horseback in 1625—since lost—met with such enthusiasm that it was displayed publicly on Madrid's main street, "to the admiration of the whole city and the envy of fellow artists." Poems were written about it, and the King granted the artist 300 ducats to cover expenses. The greatest reward of all was a life annuity of 300 ducats.

As the honors flowed in, the envy of three of Velázquez' fellow artists at court, Vincencio Carducho, Eugenio Caxés and Angelo Nardi, could no longer be contained. He was accused, among other things, of being able to paint only faces. The King decided to meet this attack on his favorite painter by putting all four painters to the test with a competition. The theme: the expulsion of the Moriscos from Spain in 1609. The Moriscos were Spaniards of Moorish descent who had been forcibly converted from Islam to Catholicism during the reign of Charles V, Philip IV's great-grandfather. But after 84 years their loyalty to Catholicism —and to Catholic Spain—was still suspect, and Philip III had them shipped to a desolate part of North Africa, where they were left to survive or die. That Philip IV wanted this event commemorated seems strange today. Although the expulsion was viewed by those who initiated it as the most humane way of dealing with these unwanted people, it was, of course, a despicable act, and it was wrongheaded, depriving Spain of as many as 500,000 of its most useful citizens, including great numbers of its farm workers and its artisans.

Philip appointed Friar Juan Bautista Maino, a painter of note who had been his drawing teacher when he was a boy, and the Roman architect Giovanni Battista Crescenzi as the judges of the competition. They had little difficulty in naming Velázquez the winner. He won with an allegorical treatment of the expulsion theme, quite out of his usual mode and far superior to his rivals' efforts. Regrettably, the picture perished, possibly in the fire that destroyed the Alcázar in 1734. But we know that it portrayed, in addition to Philip III, a crowd of weeping men, women and children, several soldiers, and "a majestic matron," Spain, holding a shield and arrows in her right hand and sheaves of grain in her left.

With his critics left to nurse their wounded pride, Velázquez was made an Usher of the Chamber on March 7, 1627, an office whose function we do not know but whose emoluments included a rent-free apartment in the city. He was also to receive a daily allowance of 12 reals, the last as a settlement for back payments owed to him by Philip's treasury, which seemed always to be in arrears. In addition, he was provided free medical care. But perhaps best and most exciting of all, he was promised a trip to the fountainhead of art, Italy. As a member of the court, he had had plenty of opportunity to examine the large collections of paintings on display in the palaces, and to develop still further his taste for the Venetians. Indeed, the King's collections had served him as a school, and he had drawn upon them for ideas to shape to his own ends. But he had learned as well as he could from them. To mature further he would have to go abroad, away from all that was familiar, to all that would be new and challenging. His intention, apparently, was to visit first Venice and survey its treasures, and then Rome, which was glorying in a resurgence of creative activity.

Velázquez' trip, however, had to be postponed; the time was not ripe. The King's long journey with Olivares to the states of Aragon, Valencia and Catalonia had left the monarch disillusioned as well as exhausted. In the summer of 1627, Philip fell desperately ill. For a while he seemed to be at death's door. The palace began to hum with intrigue. Olivares' enemies came out into the open, ready to topple the Minister. The relics of saints were brought to the King's bedside to work a cure—all to no avail. Then a monk appeared, bringing with him the "admirable and miraculous relic of the little loaves of St. Nicholas, which the King took from the hands of the friar with fervent prayers and supplication for divine help and mercy." Miraculously, the King recovered. But Philip's illness was only one of several complications that must have gotten in the way of Velázquez' trip to Italy at this time. The years 1627 and 1628 saw a steady decline in the Castilian economy. Inflation became so bad that the Crown had to devalue the currency, a move that hit private individuals hard but proved of instantaneous benefit to the royal treasury.

The postponement of the trip worked out to Velázquez' advantage in at least one way. It gave him the chance to meet the painter Peter Paul Rubens, then considered Europe's greatest artist, and a diplomat of considerable skill in the employ of Flanders. In part because of a suggestion from England, Rubens came to court from Flanders to help patch up Spanish-English relations, which had been greatly damaged by Philip's refusal to give María in marriage to Charles. He had once before visited Spain, in 1603, and had found at that time no artists worth mentioning by name in his letters. (Oddly, he ignored El Greco, then painting in Toledo.) In fact, Rubens had prayed to be delivered from those he had met, such being "the incredible incompetence and carelessness of the painters here." Now, in 1628, he was delighted to find a Spaniard of real talent, and he praised Velázquez' work for the modesty it showed. Both men seem to have gotten to know each other well, for they went together to the Escorial to examine the royal art collection.

Rubens' visit lasted from August until April, and in spite of his conferences and several attacks of gout, he managed to paint five portraits of Philip and several of the Queen and other members of the Royal Family and court. He also copied the King's Titians. How Velázquez reacted to a man of such unlimited energy and such prolific output goes unrecorded, but he seems not to have been intimidated by him in the least. Nor does he seem to have been offended when Rubens painted the King, which supposedly was Velázquez' privilege alone.

Scholars have looked hard in Velázquez' paintings for signs of Rubens' influence, but have come up with only the most insignificant of traces. Much as the painters may have liked each other, they were miles apart artistically; the one flamboyant, the other reserved. The differences in their approach to painting can be gauged from Velázquez' surviving masterpiece of this period, which is sometimes known as *The Drinkers,* or simply *Bacchus (pages 70-71).* Here was a subject Rubens would have relished: the god of wine and a satyr making merry in the company of mortals while Bacchus hands out garlands of grape leaves. Rubens would have filled his canvas with baroque energy, stroked it with lush and gorgeous color, and given to the semiclothed figures of Bacchus and the satyr the gleam and feel of fat.

Velázquez' rendition of the subject, while humorous, is entirely straightforward and earthbound, and in this it provides yet another clue to his personality. The scene takes place not in a mythological never-never land, but in Spain, with the Guadarrama Mountains in the background and a touch of the homely in the foreground, a wine jug made of rough clay. His cast of characters has been drummed up largely from the countryside; sunburned, leathery faces like these are to be seen all over Castile today. His color scheme is muted, earthy, with browns predominating. And his meaning is clear: the painting may seem to be in jest, but a beggar in the background thrusts his outstretched hand toward the carousers, a sober reminder to the 17th Century Spaniard of charity and Christ's sacrifice. Velázquez thus shows himself here to be a realist not just in manner, but in outlook. We can see him clinging to reality —and to his art—as a way of counteracting whatever effect the frenzied life of the court was having on him.

After finishing *Bacchus,* for which the King paid him 100 ducats, Velázquez began to prepare for his Italian trip. He was going at a bad time. Spain and France had come to loggerheads over control of the Duchy of Mantua, a little principality in northern Italy, and fighting had broken out. Olivares feared that French domination of Mantua would pose a serious threat to Spanish Milan and the Spanish supply route, which ran from Milan through northern Italy, Austria and Germany to Flanders. One of the cities Velázquez most wanted to see, Venice—a near neighbor of Mantua—had become a hotbed of anti-Spanish feeling over what the Venetians felt was Spain's excessive meddling in Italian affairs. To ensure Velázquez' safety and cordial welcome throughout Italy, Olivares had his Secretary of Foreign Affairs arrange through the various Italian envoys at court for letters of introduction and safe-conducts.

All this activity on behalf of an artist tended to arouse suspicion. Could Velázquez be a spy or a diplomat in disguise? One Italian emissary at the Spanish court wrote back to his patroness, the Duchess of Parma, to warn her in code that Velázquez' mission might indeed be espionage. And to support his contention, he cited the unusual treatment accorded Velázquez, a mere painter, by Philip—who watched him at work and even allowed him to paint in the royal apartments.

The King and Olivares presented the artist with money for the journey. And it was arranged that in his absence he would continue to be paid his salary. No time limit was put on the trip; he could stay as long as he liked. Velázquez sailed to Italy in the retinue of General Ambrosio Spínola, who four years before had brought Spain its most stunning victory in years, the capitulation of the reputedly impregnable Dutch city of Breda. General Spínola was being sent to Italy to take command of the Spanish troops stationed there and to assume the governorship of Milan. Velázquez must have observed the general closely on the voyage, for five years later—and four years after Spínola's death—he would immortalize this great hero's features with lifelike precision in the monumental painting *The Surrender of Breda (pages 80-81).*

Upon his arrival in Italy, Velázquez headed for Venice, where he was put up in the Spanish Ambassador's palace. So hostile were the Venetians toward Spaniards that he was given a personal bodyguard to protect him in the streets. But in spite of the troubled atmosphere, he managed to accomplish his purpose, which was to see the city's treasures and to make sketches of paintings by Titian and others of the Venetian school.

From Venice, Velázquez went to Rome, where his high connections resulted in his being installed as a guest in the Vatican Palace. There he sketched Raphael's works and Michelangelo's *Last Judgment.* He seems also to have executed at this time two enormous canvases, *The Bloody Cloak of Joseph* and *The Forge of Vulcan (page 72).* Both show an increased concern with the human figure.

Although he was obviously keeping busy, his quarters in the Vatican were somewhat out of the way, and being friendly by nature, he began to feel lonely in them. Moreover, he dreaded the heat of the Roman summer and the malaria that came with it. He asked his Roman benefactor, the Count of Monterrey, who was Olivares' brother-in-law, to intercede on his behalf and get him accommodations at the Villa Medici, on one of the city's hills. Velázquez has left us two leafy, sun-dappled views of the gardens *(pages 156 and 157).* They suggest the breezy loveliness of the place, and show us, in their loose, free brushwork, how very relaxed he became there—and how much the Venetian painters had taken hold of him with their rapturous approach to art. It was here, however, that despite his precautions he had an attack of the dreaded malaria.

After regaining his strength, and before returning home, Velázquez journeyed south to Naples at the command of Philip. The King wanted him to make a portrait of his sister María, who had been married by proxy to the King of Hungary, son of the Emperor Ferdinand II; she had interrupted her journey to Hungary for a stay in Naples. This was the same María whom the Prince of Wales—now Charles I of England —had wanted so desperately to marry.

With the portrait of María and the other works he had done in Italy in his luggage, Velázquez set sail for Spain after an absence of nearly a year and a half. When he got back to Madrid he was very well received. At Olivares' command he went to kiss the hand of His Majesty, and to thank him for having not allowed himself to be painted by anyone else.

Velázquez found waiting for him a fine new assignment. He would be the first to make a portrait of Baltasar Carlos, the little heir to the throne who had been born during his absence and gave promise of becoming a healthy, handsome boy. Providence, it seemed, was again smiling on Spain. And Spain at last had a painter of her own to record her newfound glory. The full flowering of Velázquez' genius was about to begin.

Backdrop for a Painter

On July 22, 1588, the 131 galleons of an armada that Spain regarded as invincible cleared the harbor of Corunna and headed for the English Channel to secure it —and Protestant England—for the glory of His Most Catholic Majesty Philip II, King of Castile, Aragon and Portugal, Defender of the Faith. The Spaniards had good reason for optimism. Less than a century before, Philip's great-grandparents had dispatched Christopher Columbus westward across the Atlantic; now Spain possessed gold-rich territories in the New World and had even sent an expedition halfway round the globe to plant the banner of Spain on a group of islands named, in honor of the King, the Philippines. His realms spread across Europe, and his ability to add England to the list seemed a foregone conclusion. But the Invincible Armada went down to disastrous defeat, half its ships lost to the storms of the Irish Sea and to a defensive force under Admiral Sir Francis Drake. When the news reached Philip II, he offered "Great thanks to . . . Almighty God . . . I am gifted with such power that I could easily, if I chose, place another fleet upon the sea." Nonetheless, the defeat was an omen. Spain was entering a long period of decline. While inexorably slipping from eminence, it continued to believe in its own greatness. Against this backdrop, Diego de Silva Velázquez served as court painter for Philip II's grandson, Philip IV, striving to picture reality in a world wedded to visions and dreams.

Black smoke explodes from cannon over a sea of lifeboats and flotsam in this English sketch, a design for a tapestry commemorating the repulse of the Spanish Armada. The two fleets clashed several times as the English dogged the hard-hit Spaniards through the Channel; one of the Spanish vessels is going down by the bow at upper left.

Design for a tapestry of the Armada

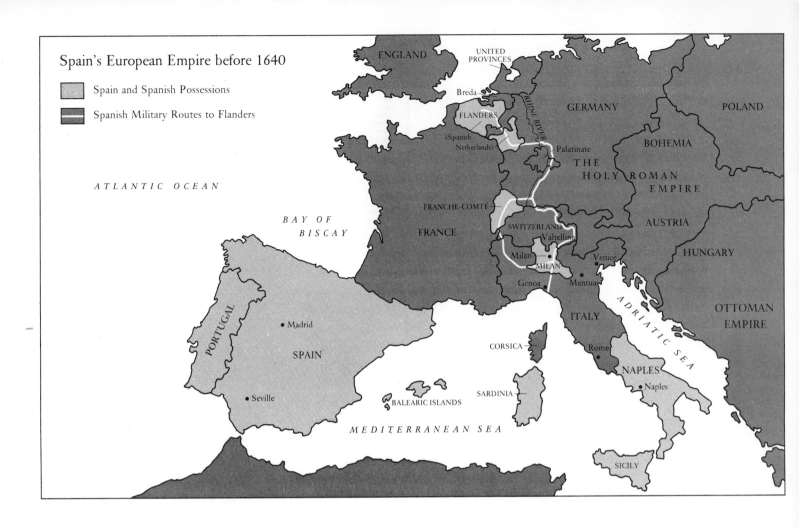

Spain's European Empire before 1640

Spain and Spanish Possessions

Spanish Military Routes to Flanders

Head of Philip II

To the austere Escorial Palace *(left)* of Philip II outside Madrid came emissaries seeking imperial favor. The more important were granted audiences with Philip II himself; the lesser caught only a glimpse of the King as he reviewed ceremonies from a distance.

Sometimes, however, visitors only thought they saw the King, for an elaborately lifelike, enameled silver head fitted into the royal armor *(above)* was often propped in Philip's place on the reviewing balcony. Philip himself usually remained closeted in two small rooms in the palace. From these quarters he attended to the empire's most picayune details himself —he even corrected the grammar in state papers in a neat script. More often, however, the royal orders concerned matters of greater moment. The King's dominions stretched from Flanders to Sicily in Europe, from Borneo to Patagonia overseas.

Military adventures helped to drain Spain's treasury. Although the empire excited Spanish pride, its potential was barely tapped. The man in the Escorial spared little time on developing the economy of his realms. Philip II was gripped by the belief that God had laid upon him and the realm an exalted role—to serve as defender of the Roman faith.

Pier Maria Baldi: *The Escorial*, late 1600s

27

Spain's wars were always holy wars. For 80 years Spanish troops fought and died to keep the Protestant Netherlands bound to the empire. The bitter, protracted struggle is here depicted in an allegorical painting entitled *Fishing for Souls* by the Dutch artist Adriaen van der Veen. In this clash of faiths, soberly garbed Dutch

Protestants on the left confront Spanish Catholics on the right, as partisans of both sides attempt to capture recruits for their respective causes from the river between them.

Among the Catholic forces, leaning on a cane in the small clearing at far right, is Philip III, who succeeded Philip II in 1598. Spain's new monarch was by no means

Adriaen Pietersz van de Venne: *Fishing for Souls*, c. 1614

as formidable a figure as his father. But even if he held the reins of empire less firmly, he was just as militant a champion of Catholicism. Philip III tenaciously pursued the war against the Dutch until 1609, when financial and military reverses compelled him to agree to a truce —which proved only temporary.

In the Netherlands and elsewhere on the Continent a rising tide of social, economic and political change promised to transform society and lead Europe out of medievalism. Spain expended all of its power fighting this spirit of change, defending an ephemeral ideal of noble pride and faith that was wedded to the past.

If Spain's rulers did not always realize the extent of the realm's decay, some Spanish artists appeared to. Their work began to reflect a wistful, melancholy mood called *desengaño*—disillusionment. Antonio de Pereda epitomized it in *The Dream of Life*, which shows jewels, gold coins, carnival masks, crowns and a globe—symbols of Spanish glory—heaped in a sorry pile, inevitably to vanish when the dreaming figure of Spain awakens.

This was the country's mood after Philip III was succeeded by Philip IV in 1621—the reign during which

30

Antonio de Pereda: *The Dream of Life, c. 1655*

Velázquez painted. With each passing year disaster added to disaster. The country was continually plagued by war. An entire treasure fleet was seized by pirates in 1628. Two years later Brazil fell to the Dutch. The 1640s were a decade of famine, culminating in the great plague of 1648-1649, in which thousands of Spaniards perished.

Thus Spain's power gradually dwindled as the years wore on. But as the country continued to cling to its illusions, its prideful spirit remained—a spirit that Velázquez was brilliantly to record for posterity.

32

II

Beginning
with Success

Few are the artists who have achieved so much so early as Velázquez. He became painter to the King at a point in his life when other men often are still trying out their talent. In accounting for his success at court, it could be said that he was the right man at the right time in the right place. He happened along when he was needed, and his sober realism exactly matched the serious intent of Spain's new regime. Yet this is not enough to explain the esteem in which he came to be held by the King. Even his teacher and father-in-law, Pacheco, found Philip IV's generosity to Velázquez remarkable. What was it, then, that raised him to such heights of royal favor? One factor was of course the enormous talent that set him apart from his fellow painters, but how did he bring it to fruition? Where did he develop it? What are the origins of this towering figure in the world of Spanish art?

The record is tantalizingly incomplete. Practically the only thing we know with any certainty about him before the age of 12 is that he was reared in a genteel home. But it is an important fact. His parents, Juan Rodriguez de Silva and Jerónima Velázquez, belonged to the hidalgo class, the lowest order of nobility, from whose ranks traditionally had come the lawyers, professional soldiers, clerics and administrators of the realm. This was a heterogeneous group: some hidalgos were poor, some rich; some were of ancient families, while others had only recently been titled. But what they all held in common was a contempt for commerce and a refusal to do manual labor. Even the poorest of them were immensely proud. They lived by, and for, honor, hoping to distinguish themselves through the virtues of their class—loyalty, courage and generosity. The fact that so little is known about Velázquez in Seville and at the court probably reflects to his credit; it could be a sign that he led a life above reproach, a life of true honor. He was never someone to gossip about.

Velázquez' heritage, in addition to being a proud one, was further enhanced by its being an old one—an advantage not all hidalgos enjoyed, especially in an age when patents of nobility were readily sold by the Crown as a means of raising desperately needed money. The De Silvas, his father's family, claimed descent from the Portuguese aristocracy, but

This tender religious scene was among Velázquez' first commissioned works, probably painted for a Seville church when the artist was only 20. His talent for portraiture is already apparent in the lifelike treatment of the faces of the wise men surrounding the Madonna and the Christ Child. Over the years the picture has suffered: it has darkened, and its sides have been cut down.

The Adoration of the Magi, 1619

they had come down in the world and were left, as Palomino, Velázquez' 18th Century biographer, politely put it, with no other resources than "their advantages and their valor." His mother's people were Sevillians, endowed, it was also said, "with virtue, rank and nobility." But toward the end of his career, when Velázquez was being considered for knighthood, the purity of their blood could not be established without a shadow of a doubt, and no less a personage than Pope Alexander VII had to waive the requirement that proof be presented of noble birth on both sides of the family. Only then was Velázquez able to become a knight of the Order of Santiago, and allowed to wear the Order's emblem, the red cross that can be seen stitched to his black blouse in *Las Meninas.*

The exact date of Velázquez' birth in Seville is lost; we have only the date of his baptism, June 6, 1599, but it is presumed that he was born in the same month. The oldest of seven children, he was christened Diego, possibly after an Andalusian saint who had had a hand in converting some of the Moors, and the boy grew up as Diego Velázquez. It was not unusual in Andalusia, of which Seville is the capital, for the male child to be given for his last name his mother's maiden name; this was often done to encourage a legacy from the maternal grandparents. Not until the 1640s, when the artist was deeply involved in the life of the court, did he prefer to be known as Diego de Silva Velázquez, which apparently had a more prestigious ring to it.

In some ways, Velázquez could not have been born at a worse time. Famine and plague were sweeping through Andalusia and Castile. Economic life was at a standstill and there seemed little chance that it would recover soon. Taxes, rents and Church tithes had left thousands of people bankrupt and driven thousands of others overseas. Whole villages stood half-empty and roads swarmed with 150,000 vagabonds, beggars, thieves and prostitutes in a land of only six million. The middle class had practically ceased to exist—and this in an age when trade and finance were contributing to the emergence of a small but strong bourgeoisie in France, England and Holland. The upper classes and the Church were parasites upon the country. Because it was a matter of pride with the hidalgos and nobles never to work with their hands, laborers and artisans had to be imported from abroad to perform the tasks that poor aristocratic Spaniards refused to do. Good jobs were scarce. The religious orders began to fill up with the unemployed. As monks and nuns the wellborn could at least continue to live with their pretensions.

However bleak the times, Velázquez was blessed in at least one respect —he was born in Seville. It was a city of ancient and proud heritage, built upon successive layers of Roman, Visigothic, Moorish and Spanish culture. It was also a city of great beauty and cultivation—"the most famous city upon which the sun shines," in the words of a contemporary. And it still had wealth. Situated 50 miles up the Guadalquivir River from the Mediterranean, it was Spain's busiest port, a funnel through which the gold and silver of the colonies in the New World poured, either on the way to the royal treasury or, more often, to bankers in other parts of Europe to whom the Crown was royally in debt. The population of Seville had surged to 150,000 in 1598, more than Madrid's,

The gold and silver that supported Spanish power flowed from New World towns like the mining center of Castrovirreina, shown in this 1613 drawing from a book by a Peruvian Indian. From diggings high in the Andes, miners led llamas down steep trails to the church-dominated village center, where the metal was packed for shipment to the sea. The flow of treasure from such towns reached its peak around 1590, but by about 1600 it had ebbed. By then the mines had become costlier to operate, especially after an epidemic decimated the Indian labor force; soon English and Dutch competition began to nibble greedily at Spanish control over the Americas, and the foundation of Spain's glory slowly crumbled.

and included many foreigners who inhabited colorful quarters of their own. Italians living there found Seville most like one of their own cities because of its *brio,* its spirit.

In its architecture and customs, Seville was an exotic blend of Moorish and Spanish influences. Many women still followed the ancient habit of concealing their faces behind veils, and when their menfolk were away at sea, they gave the city the look of a harem. The city's great cathedral, the largest in Christendom, had for its bell tower the minaret of the mosque that once had occupied the cathedral's site. Almost within the shadow of the tower lay the Alcázar, a Moorish palace of lacy openwork surrounded by semitropical gardens redolent of jasmine. And in the manner of a North African city, Seville's houses huddled together and gleamed white under the bleaching sun. Between them ran streets narrow and twisting; doorways opened up on cool whitewashed patios with splashing fountains and potted plants. The novelist Cervantes wrote that in Seville more adventures could be found "in every street and round every corner than can be met with in any other place."

Seville prided itself on its sophistication; it was less a city of Spain than a city of the world. Sevillians of good breeding upheld as their ideal that of the Renaissance man, and they strove to be as accomplished in as many matters of the mind as possible. They followed the example of the 15th Century Florentines and met together in informal academies to discuss ideas and extend guidance to any member who might be engaged in a literary or artistic project. Reflecting their humanistic interests, their homes contained numerous art treasures—many brought from abroad. There were few more beautiful palaces anywhere in Spain than that of the Dukes of Alcalá, the Casa de Pilatos, with its tiled rooms and patios and its collections of jewels, coins, books, paintings and antique sculpture—which Velázquez may have sketched during his apprentice days.

Art flourished in Seville and artists seemed never to lack commissions. The Church, erecting one monastic house after another, was a major patron. The city had become a magnet for talent, and painters and sculptors came from all over Europe to work there, including, in the 16th Century, Pietro Torrigiano, the hot-tempered sculptor who had broken Michelangelo's nose during an argument when both were students in Florence. By Velázquez' day artists occupied their own quarter, the Triana, just across the river from the Torre del Oro, the fortified tower where the gold and silver of the treasure fleets were stored.

There was an even more flourishing market for the artists' work in the colonies, and this of course they could easily supply; the galleons to transport their pictures and altarpieces lay right at their doorsteps. At times the demand from abroad must have been almost too much of a good thing. One artist accepted a commission from Veracruz, Mexico, for 12 portraits of members of the reigning houses of Spain and Austria, 24 portraits of Holy Roman emperors and 14 of French peers, plus an assortment of religious pictures. Not surprisingly, versatility as well as speed became the hallmarks of Seville's painters.

For Velázquez, whose talent asserted itself early, the career of an artist must have seemed an attractive one, and all the more so because of the al-

A ship of Spain's busy Silver Fleet, which carried the New World's bounties home, is pictured on this ceramic tile, once used as ceiling decoration. The rendering is not very accurate, greatly exaggerating the elevation of stern and prow. This distinctive configuration is, however, typical of the galleons that sailed in *flotas,* or fleets, convoyed by six or eight armed vessels. *Flotas* left twice a year from the southern Spanish ports of Seville and Cádiz, carrying grain, oil, cloth and wine for the colonists overseas. When the ships docked at Veracruz, Cartagena or Nombre de Dios these necessities were unloaded, and replaced by the precious cargoes of silver and gold that Spain craved so desperately.

Towering nearly a hundred yards into the sky, the Moorish minaret beside Seville's cathedral was four centuries old by Velázquez' time. Partly covered with glazed tiles, it is still Seville's chief landmark. In 1176 Moslem engineers built the huge tower—scaled so that a man could ride horseback within it all the way to the top. During the Renaissance, a belfry and a bronze statue of Faith that pivoted as a weather vane were added, inspiring the popular name for the tower, Giralda—from the Spanish verb *"girar,"* meaning "to turn."

ternatives—the bureaucracy or the Church. He was a bright boy and a brilliant student. He shone in languages, philosophy and painting. Apparently his proud parents felt no qualms over his becoming a painter, since art was regarded in Spain as a profession carrying a certain dignity. According to his biographer Palomino, they turned him over to Francisco de Herrera the Elder, "a strict man, little given to charity, but of very good taste in painting and in other arts."

Here a minor mystery arises. Although Palomino credits Herrera with having been Velázquez' first teacher, this story is flatly denied by Velázquez' principal instructor, Pacheco. In *The Art of Painting,* he brooks no claim but his own, and specifically states that he gave the boy "five years of education and training." He confesses however to outrage over the "audacity" of someone—whom he deliberately does not name—who wanted to share the honor of having taught Velázquez, "the crown of my old age." What happened may have been this: The contract with Pacheco for Velázquez' apprenticeship was signed in September 1611, apparently some time after training had actually begun, for it stipulates that six years of training were to commence on December 1, 1610. Pacheco, however, was away from Seville through the winter of 1610 and 1611. During this period, he may have turned the boy over to an assistant or another artist—who could have been Herrera, whom he had once taught. If so, it is easy to understand that a proud master like Pacheco would have been reluctant to give a share of credit for Velázquez' eventual success to a former pupil.

What influence Herrera exercised over Velázquez—if any at all—cannot be gauged. He was nonetheless an artist of considerable talent. Over his lifetime he built a solid reputation as a painter of religious scenes and genre subjects, but also acquired a reputation as a man of fiery temperament, and Velázquez may have been well rid of him. His own children were supposed to have been so afraid of his anger that they left home, a daughter to enter a convent, a son to run off to Italy.

Pacheco was a very different sort, a good and gentle man and, from all accounts, an excellent teacher. He taught Velázquez a great deal. And though he was very much a didactic artist, he seems to have encouraged his young pupil to experiment. Soon Velázquez rose above his master's precepts—and apparently even became an influence on him.

Pacheco was one of Seville's leading citizens as well as one of its most prominent artists. His uncle had been a canon of the cathedral and from him Pacheco inherited the academy that did so much to add luster to his name. In 1618 he was made a censor and examiner of religious paintings for Seville's Holy Inquisition, the man who saw to it that fellow artists did not overstep the bounds of good taste or allow anything of a heretical nature to creep into their works. His views on art were widely respected, and as the author of several books and "very elegant verse" on the subject, he won the acclaim of "all the writers of his time."

If Pacheco had one fault, it is a big one in posterity's judgment. He was not a very good artist. But only a few of his contemporaries seem to have been aware of this. Among these few was the wit who penned the following poem after seeing a Crucifixion Pacheco had done:

Who made thee thus, oh Lord,
So insipid and so dry?
Love, thou wilt say is the word
But Pacheco did it, say I.

"Dry" is the word that often crops up in descriptions of Pacheco's work. Most of his surviving paintings are of religious subjects, and they show clear signs of having been approached religiously; yet they are without any life at all. Although Pacheco bridged the 16th and 17th Centuries (he was 80 when he died in 1644), his artistic roots were planted all too deeply in the 16th Century, when first Flemish paintings and then "Romanism" had held sway in Spain. The latter, the outgrowth of Michelangelo's late style, combined with the influences from Flanders, did much to give his work its stilted quality.

In his thinking Pacheco was not much more modern than in his painting. He reflected the strong influence of the Council of Trent. This august body had met off and on between 1545 and 1563 to discuss Church reform in the face of the Protestant revolution. During the Council's closing sessions certain principles had been laid down for artists painting religious scenes, and these Pacheco embraced as his own. Art was to be the handmaiden of the Church, purged of all traces of secularism and heresy. Artists were to resist flights of fancy and concentrate on Biblical texts. The texts were to be followed exactly unless a particular passage lacked sufficient detail to go by; then painters could use their imaginations, but only within the circumscribed limits of holy doctrine. Beauty that did not offend chaste and pious eyes was encouraged, but truth was to take precedence over it and to be expressed even if the effect was unpleasant. Thus an artist portraying the flagellation of Christ would be expected to show Christ "afflicted, bleeding, spat upon, with His skin torn, wounded, deformed, pale and unsightly."

Pacheco took pride in his knowledge of Church doctrine and eagerly applied it to what he felt were the problems facing the artists of his day. Burning issues for him included such questions as: Was Christ to be shown crucified with three nails or four? Was the Virgin to be depicted as a child learning to read, when it seemed likely that God would have endowed her with this skill? Were her feet to be painted uncovered or covered? In *The Art of Painting,* Pacheco spelled out in great detail how different religious themes were to be treated. He gave, for example, a complete set of instructions for painting Mary as the Virgin of the Immaculate Conception, the dogma that she was conceived free of original sin.

Lest anyone disregard his views as personal ones, Pacheco prefaced his remarks with a reminder that the version "I follow is the one most in accord with the holy revelation of the Evangelist [John], and approved by the Catholic Church with the authority of the sacred and holy interpreters." Thus there could be little deviation from Pacheco's formula —and from the looks of pictures done around this time, there wasn't.

"The Virgin of the Immaculate Conception must be painted in the flower of her youth, 12 or 13 years old, as a most beautiful young girl, with fine and serious eyes, a most perfect nose and mouth and pink cheeks, wearing her most beautiful golden hair loose." She should have on a "white tunic and blue mantle," and behind her should be the sun, "an oval sun of ocher and white that surrounds the whole image, gently fusing it to the sky." She is to be crowned by stars, "twelve stars arranged in a distinct circle amid rays coming from her sacred forehead," and the stars are to be painted as "very clear spots of purest white." She must stand on a crescent moon—but one with the tips pointed down rather than sideways. In *The Art of Painting,* Pacheco was not above citing his own representations of the Immaculate Conception as being among the best treatments of the theme. But he permitted himself a little aside that gives the text a redeeming charm and makes him seem almost human. "[In my painting] I forgot the dragon, the common enemy, whose head the Virgin broke when she triumphed over original sin. I always forget it quite naturally. The truth is that I always paint it much against my will and I shall omit it whenever I can, in order not to embarrass my painting."

Pacheco believed that art's greatest function was the uplifting of men's souls; he saw excellent painting as encouraging virtuous living. But this was a belief that could lead to difficulties. How, for example, were beautiful women to be painted without inciting lust in the beholder? "Here is what I would do," says Pacheco in that positive manner of his. "I would take the faces and hands of virtuous women from life. And for the remaining parts I would make use of good paintings, prints and drawings, ancient and modern statues." By ignoring the flesh, Pacheco hoped to produce a correct, yet proper image—and thus avoid "the danger."

We do not of course know the reactions of the young Velázquez to all this. He was only 12 when he came to Pacheco's studio to live and work. By the terms of his contract he was to get room and board and a complete set of new clothing—including a pair of shoes, breeches, two jackets, two shirts, stockings, a cape, a hat and a belt. And he was to be taken care of by Pacheco if he became ill, for a period of up to 15 days. In addition, he would receive training as an artist and something else as well, something very important to a hidalgo, an education.

That education came easily in Pacheco's workshop. It was in the very air Velázquez breathed. The ideas that Pacheco discussed with the writers and theoreticians of Seville must have excited the boy's intellect. The recognition he received from these men, the leading lights of the community, undoubtedly bolstered his confidence. And he was young enough —and bright enough—not to be taken in by all he heard; he survived Pacheco's pedantry. Meanwhile, his intelligence got the kind of workout that sharpened and focused it. In part because of the initial stimulation given it in this "gilded cage of the arts," it remained restlessly active until the end of his life. An inventory of Velázquez' library made after his death showed that he owned, in addition to numerous works on art and architecture, books by philosophers, poets and social observers such as Aristotle, Horace, Petrarch, Ariosto and Castiglione, half a dozen volumes relating to astrology, nearly 20 on astronomy, maps and explorations, as well as others dealing with mathematics, medicine, mechanics, horsemanship, ballistics and archeology.

As his books suggest—and his paintings make abundantly clear—his was a disciplined mind, a selective one. He found his inspiration in the pursuit of reality. The challenge for him lay in making everything he painted real—making the people in his pictures breathe. And here can indeed be felt the influence of Pacheco.

Pacheco was a hard and driving master. He put his students through a rigorous course in drawing and probably urged them, as he did other artists in *The Art of Painting*, to finish their sketches in one sitting in order to keep the effect spontaneous. He preferred them to work from live models and real objects, and he insisted that they pay attention to the slightest details—not just to the folds and creases of the model's draperies but to the look and feel of the cloth itself. He valued three-dimensionality more than beauty. If a picture possessed strength and "seemed round like a solid object and natural and deceived the eyes as if it were coming out of the frame," then it satisfied Pacheco. He firmly believed that a portrait should be more than a likeness of the sitter; it should spring to life.

In *The Art of Painting*, Pacheco describes the lengths to which Velázquez went to achieve perfection in portraiture. He would bribe—that is Pacheco's word—a peasant boy to sit for him, and sketch him on sheets of blue paper in various poses—"now crying, now laughing." While this practice tells us something about Velázquez' precocity and early dedication to his career, it also reveals how independent he was even as a student. He was obviously ambitious; he struck out on his own when he hired that peasant boy, and soon, proud young hidalgo that he was, he managed to do what other artists often take years to accomplish —he turned his back on his teacher's style. Perhaps the biggest single influence on him at this time was the realistic art of the Italian painter Caravaggio. Velázquez may have seen paintings by him in Seville, or at least copies of the Italian's works.

During the early 17th Century, Caravaggism was a strong wind blowing through Europe, and Velázquez would have felt its effect even without being exposed to a single one of Caravaggio's pictures. What Caravaggio did was to revolutionize painting by demonstrating that the ordinary could be raised to the level of art and enjoyed in its own right. And he rendered his realistic scenes in an intense, clear light, which made for strong, hard shadows. "He came upon the scene," wrote the Italian Pietro Bellori in 1672, "at a time when realism was not much in fashion and when figures were made according to convention and manner and satisfied more the taste for gracefulness than for truth."

Velázquez certainly had a taste for truth. When asked in later years why he had not tried to raise the level of his art to that of Raphael, he replied that he preferred to be "first in the common, rather than second in the sublime." As a student, he deliberately chose to do much of his work in a humble genre, the *bodegón*, the peculiarly Spanish version of the still life. *Bodegón* means "low eating place," and paintings of this type showed not only food and drink, but plain people making merry in plain settings. The genre's popularity in the first quarter of the 17th Century was paralleled in literature by a vogue for picaresque novels, the warm and human adventures of simple types who lived by their wits.

But here again Velázquez asserted his independence. Unlike contemporary *bodegones,* his best do more than amuse; they seize the mind with the force of their meaning. And while showing how much he learned from Caravaggio's example, they also demonstrate that he was no slavish disciple of the Italian. He had his own thoughts about light and his own definite ideas of what was natural, and he put all of them to work. Through his *bodegones,* says Pacheco, he came to find "the true imitation of nature."

Examining these fascinating paintings, it is possible to chart Velázquez' development—actually to see him gaining that self-assurance, that sureness of touch, that faithfulness to a visual experience that would enable him one day to plunge beneath the surface of things. Among the first of the *bodegones* are *Three Men at a Table, A Girl and Two Men at Table* and *Musical Trio.* Nobody could fail to identify them as early works. The figures seem hemmed in by the narrow space allotted them, and they relate unnaturally to one another as they sit or stand around a table. There is an overconcern with detail. Yet many of the figures are well characterized, objects have been chosen and arranged with a selective eye, and the colors are handsomely muted.

S till, the promise shown here is hardly enough to account for the enormous maturity shown by the 19-year-old Velázquez in his first great *bodegón, The Old Woman Frying Eggs* of 1618 *(page 45),* which has the spare look and dignity that forever afterward were to be identified with his work. The painting is as direct as its title. Seen in profile, with her head wrapped in a white shawl, the old woman has just broken two eggs into a clay cooking vessel. As she waits for them to congeal, her thoughts drift off. Behind her and to the left stands a similarly self-absorbed boy, holding a melon in one hand and a flask in the other. The effect is of arrested motion, of pervasive silence, two qualities that 38 years later *Las Meninas* would exhibit so powerfully. But still there is a world of difference between that late painting and this early one. Although Velázquez obviously took deep pleasure in rendering the nuances of light on all the humble objects in the foreground and background—the pitchers, the bowls, even the string tied around the melon—he was still a long way from utilizing light to create an almost palpable sense of depth in the grand manner of *Las Meninas.* Instead, he used it here dramatically, letting it shine in from some source outside the painting and high to the left. It cuts through the cool darkness of the room to illuminate the woman and boy and create sharp shadows, and as it does so, it sets the edges of things to gleaming and the whites everywhere to glowing. And much as Velázquez demonstrated here how he loved paint—spreading it onto his canvas with thick, moist strokes of his brush and allowing the surging rhythms of these strokes to reinforce the contours of the woman's dress—he was still many years away from the splendid looseness of touch, the thin, exquisite application of pigment to canvas that is his trait and that has led some people to compare his oil technique to that of a watercolorist. Nonetheless, *The Old Woman Frying Eggs* is a phenomenon: in its simplicity, in its restraint, in its purity, it exudes a spirituality.

Two other remarkable paintings done somewhat later speak eloquently of Velázquez' continued concern with the humble. They are *The Waterseller* and *Two Young Men at a Table*. In the latter no attempt was made to characterize the youths: one has his back to the viewer, the other his head lowered. They are there—along with the jugs, the mortar and pestle, the stacked, overturned plates—only as shapes to be molded by Velázquez' soft yet penetrating light. But now his light seems less an isolating force and more a unifying one; it ties things together, unites them in one atmosphere.

As much as I am stirred by this painting, I prefer *The Waterseller (page 47)*. I had seen it many times in reproduction, but I was totally unprepared for its stillness the first time I stood before it. I found myself almost listening to it. Here, in a permanent state of equilibrium, enclosed in the parabola formed by their bodies, are three figures: the water seller; a boy accepting from him an enormous glass of water freshened with a fig; and in the background, obscured by shadow, someone drinking. The gazes of the man and boy are turned inward, almost as though an act of ritual significance were being performed, and even the dimpled clay jugs, down one of which water coolly trickles, appear to be more than ordinary objects as Velázquez' light bites into them and defines, with haunting precision, every little dent in their surfaces. The effect is of heightened reality, of a second made to exist forever. Although *The Waterseller* may have no extraordinary meaning, it speaks so eloquently of Velázquez' fresh vision and of the reverence with which he had already come to view life that it can seem to contain a meaning.

The people of Velázquez' *bodegones* are eminently real. We do not stop to wonder who they were; they exist before us, and that is enough. But in the case of *The Waterseller,* we actually know who the man was, and what we know increases our understanding of Velázquez' so-called naturalism. The model for the central figure was indeed a water seller, a familiar character around Seville known as El Corso, The Corsican. Velázquez chose to portray El Corso as a man of dignity, ennobled by his work, with life creased deeply in his face. According to one source, El Corso seems to have been quite another type. He wore a smock all right, but a dirty, ragged one, and through its rips and tears people could see scabs and calluses on his chest and abdomen. Velázquez tempered his realism; he may have ignored the sublime, but he did not seek out the ugly.

Velázquez' life, even in these early years, was that of a very successful man. After finishing his training with Pacheco and passing a qualifying examination, he was admitted early in 1617 to the painters' guild. As a fully accredited artist, he could now hire an assistant, have his own studio and accept commissions. Perhaps being on his own helped trigger off the greatness first seen in *The Old Woman Frying Eggs*. In his personal life he was lucky too. "Moved by his virtue, purity of blood, and good parts, and by the hopes of his natural and great intellect," Pacheco gave him his daughter Juana in marriage in 1618. The couple was well off; Juana's dowry included real estate, and Velázquez' ability assured them a living. A year later, their first child, Francisca, was born (of the two children of this union, both girls, Francisca alone would survive childhood).

This unusually expressive painted wooden crucifix, made about 1603 by Juan Martínez Montañés, evidently exerted a strong influence on the young artists in Seville, including Velázquez. The sculptor admirably fulfilled the terms of his contract for the work, which specified that Christ was to be shown alive, "looking toward whomsoever should be praying at His feet, so that it will appear that Christ Himself addresses him, saying that it is for him that He suffers thus." Velázquez became a good friend of the sculptor, whose portrait he painted, and he reveals in his own powerful *Crucifixion (page 53)* his debt to this work, especially in the treatment of Christ's head and eyes.

CATHEDRAL OF SEVILLE

Velázquez continued to explore the rich possibilities offered by the *bodegón* for coming to grips with reality. Now for the first time his pictures of this type clearly expressed a meaning, and the message was a religious one, in keeping with Pacheco's basic tenet, the central point of *The Art of Painting*—that "the aim of painting is the service of God." There is no mistaking the moral of *Christ in the House of Martha and Mary (pages 48-49)*. But although the tone may be more consciously elevated here than in previous works, the approach is still as direct as ever. At first glance the painting seems nothing more than a kitchen scene, an ordinary *bodegón.* An old woman and a servant girl with red, work-worn hands occupy part of the foreground, and on a table beside them are various objects—a plate with fish, another plate with eggs, a jug, a few cloves of garlic, a pepper. The old woman is admonishing the maid for her reluctance to get on with the dinner. But as she does so, she points toward the back of the room, to what looks like a picture on the wall but which could also be a mirror or a window—an ambiguity scholars have spent no small amount of time trying to straighten out. Seen within the frame of the picture-mirror-window is Christ seated, with Mary at His feet and Martha standing by. This is the key with which to unlock the meaning of the painting.

Martha and Mary were sisters of Lazarus. They entertained Jesus in their home. Mary, whose duty it should have been to help serve, chose instead to sit at the feet of Jesus and to listen to His teachings. This annoyed Martha. Bothered by having to serve, she came to Jesus and said, "Lord, dost thou not care that my sister hath left me to serve alone? Bid her therefore that she help me." And Jesus answered and said to her, "Martha, Martha, thou art careful and troubled about many things. But one thing is needful; and Mary hath chosen that good part, which shall not be taken away from her." Subsequently Martha was to choose that good part too—and follow Christ. The old woman, in pointing to the Biblical scene, apparently is reminding the girl that she would do well to imitate Martha's and Mary's example—and put Christ ahead of herself and before any man. But the ways of serving Christ are many, she seems to be saying, and one is work, diligence to duty, for which there will be a reward in the life to come. In this there is a strong echo of a statement by St. Paul that Pacheco used with emphasis in *The Art of Painting* to underscore the artist's role: "Servants, obey in all things your masters. . . . And whatever you do, do it heartily, as to the Lord, and not unto men . . . for ye serve the Lord Christ."

Christ in the House of Martha and Mary is both a secular and religious painting, and was probably meant to hang in a home. But even in the works he had begun to do for the Church Velázquez remained a realist. His view of the world of the spirit was informed by what he knew of the world of the flesh, and accordingly he painted Biblical scenes in human terms. Yet never was he irreverent. One of his earliest purely religious paintings is *The Adoration of the Magi (page 32).* As a yellow dawn breaks in a black sky, the wise men huddle around the Christ Child. And what a beautiful baby the little Jesus is—a real baby, filled with the radiant freshness of infancy. Mary is no less real. She is proud of her lovely Child. The warmth expressed here may have had to do with the fact that around this time Velázquez became a father. Some scholars have suggested that Juana, his wife, and Francisca, their firstborn, served as his models.

The supple poetry of *The Adoration* is intensified to revelation in two other religious paintings of perhaps the same year, *The Immaculate Conception* and *St. John Writing the Apocalypse (pages 50 and 51),* which were meant to hang together in a room of a convent. Velázquez, still beholden to his master, followed Pacheco's formula for treating the Immaculate Conception almost to the letter. His Virgin is a girl of 12 or 13, "in the flower of her youth." And, just as in Pacheco's description, she stands on a crescent moon, backed up by the sun, with a crown of stars sparkling above loose, golden hair. But Velázquez' painting has a three-dimensionality, a reality, that Pacheco's does not, and it contains none of his master's simpering sweetness. So natural a view of the supernatural may reflect a concept prevalent in Velázquez' day. This held that God portrayed Himself in His greatest works and that the painter who imitated nature was imitating God. Apparently it was enough for Velázquez to use a live model for his Virgin, and to paint her well.

St. John Writing the Apocalypse, the companion work to *The Immaculate Conception,* follows in the same realistic vein. Velázquez' saint is no withered ascetic, but a strong man with a heavy face and full, sensual lips. Only his eyes give away the ecstasy he feels as he looks up from his manuscript and confronts an apocalyptic vision in the sky—a dragon and a woman with wings. Velázquez handled the vision well, certainly, but he did not allow it to overwhelm his painting. Indeed, he paid every bit as much attention to the dog-eared books that lie at the saint's feet and constitute a beautiful little still life of their own. Velázquez, it would seem, was much less interested in exploiting the miraculous than in the sense of mystery to be gained from painting moonlight. A cool opalescent sheen bathes the saint. He stands out against the darkness, a figure of lonely and powerful isolation.

From such paintings and the scraps of fact we know about Velázquez during his Sevillian years, we can sense what motivated him. He was enormously able but he had the ambitious pride of a hidalgo. He was not content simply to follow the tried and the acceptable. He wanted to be at the top. Had he decided to stay in Seville, he could easily have become its foremost religious painter. But by the 1620s, Seville's days of greatness were numbered, and there must have been signs all around of the decay that would soon turn the city into a backwater. The Guadalquivir had always been difficult to navigate and now, as ships became bigger, the problem was accentuated. To complicate matters, the river was beginning to silt up. More and more trade would be diverted to Cádiz. Realist that we know him to be, Velázquez may have been aware of all this, and perhaps it increased his determination to go to Madrid. But there was something else that spurred him on: the chance to live close to power, to live as a hidalgo among others of his class. When at last he left Seville, he went forth not just as a painter confident of his own abilities, but as a gentleman possessing the all-important grace and dignity that would make him more than a servant in the King's eyes.

It is not uncommon for a pupil to outdo his teacher in art, but seldom is a teacher actually inspired by his protégé, as Pacheco was by Velázquez. In at least two works—a drawing *(above)* and a painting—Pacheco emulated his son-in-law and pupil. The older man wrote of having painted a *bodegón* scene in the natural and lifelike manner of Velázquez and later finding that in its presence the rest of his own works seemed merely painted. Pacheco's pen-and-wash drawing above was probably influenced by a painting *(page 51)* Velázquez had completed some 14 years earlier. Unlike Pacheco's other work, this near-copy is free and spontaneous.

A Taste for Truth

Diego Velázquez, like many another great painter, proved his genius early. Apprenticed to a Seville artist at 11, he was accepted into the artists' guild six years later and was painting masterpieces at 19—masterpieces of enormous skill, revealing the self-confidence and control characteristic of a mature artist. His achievement at so young an age is all the more remarkable for the fact that he broke with tradition; for decades Spanish painters had been imitators of the Flemish and Italian schools. Velázquez refused to follow this well-trodden path, but neither did he make the mistake of abandoning tradition. With a sure sense for the limits acceptable to his audience, he breathed life and spirit into the largely moribund art of Spain. He first attracted attention with his *bodegones*, still lifes that included people—a highly popular type of painting in 17th Century Spain. Velázquez' *bodegones* were fresh: realistic yet restrained. These qualities, traits that were to characterize all of Velázquez' work, also distinguish his early religious paintings. Their excellence was quickly recognized in his native city, but in a typical show of assurance, Velázquez turned his back on a potentially successful career as a painter of religious themes and left Seville to establish himself at the Madrid court. He was then just 24 years old. But even if he had stopped painting at this time, these early accomplishments in Seville would still have earned him lasting honor in the annals of art.

In this work, executed when Velázquez was 19, the artist met the requirements of the 17th Century *bodegón*: ordinary people are shown with objects associated with food. But he lifted this painting above the level of the routine *bodegón* by his careful attention to detail and the sense of immediacy he conveyed. The woman and boy break off in mid-conversation; the eggs are caught in the very act of congealing. Considered Velázquez' first masterpiece, *The Old Woman Frying Eggs* displays the persuasiveness that was to pervade and enliven all his later work.

The Old Woman Frying Eggs, 1618

The Waterseller, c. 1619-1620

Velázquez was about 20 when he completed *The Waterseller* (*above, detail at left*), a *bodegón* that helped secure his reputation in Seville. The model for the work, familiar to Sevillians, was El Corso, The Corsican, one of many men who sold fresh water on the dusty streets of the southern city. Relentless heat made water sellers an absolute necessity in the arid summers. Neighborhood pumps often went dry, and even when they did not, their water was never as refreshing as that sold by the street vendors. The water was kept cool in clay jugs and often flavored by the addition of a sweet fig or an aromatic herb such as fennel or rosemary. Velázquez' painting captures the sense of temporary rest and refreshment. The artist also reveals a preoccupation with an orderly arrangement of forms; the figures are carefully placed in a parabola that complements the graceful curves of the water jugs. The jugs themselves are a triumph. Every dip and bulge in their surfaces is caught in highlight or shadow; the large water jug in the foreground seems so real that its water-spattered curves appear to project from the canvas.

The most distinctive of the religious scenes Velázquez produced before he left Seville is *Christ in the House of Martha and Mary*, in which the artist combined elements of the *bodegón* with a Biblical theme. The subject is simple: an old woman points to a scene showing Jesus teaching Martha and Mary. She seems to be telling the girl to heed Jesus, choose Him over all others and serve Him by working. The utensils, fish, eggs, garlic cloves

Christ in the House of Martha and Mary, c. 1618

and jug are so expertly rendered that they constitute a still life by themselves. Once again, as in *The Old Woman Frying Eggs,* the characters appear to have been suspended in time. But there is also an added touch of mystery.

Velázquez has left unanswered an intriguing question about the bright vignette of Jesus and His listeners. Is it a picture on the wall of the room, a reflection in a mirror, or a glimpse through a window?

The Immaculate Conception, c. 1619

Among Velázquez' first religious works were these two paintings. Both are singular demonstrations of how well he adapted his skill to the often strict demands of Spanish religious art. The paintings had to conform to iconographic standards, but Velázquez took inspired artistic liberties. The Virgin Mary *(above)* is painted to satisfy some of the rules: 12 stars surround her head, her feet are modestly covered, and she stands on a crescent

St. John Writing the Apocalypse, 1619

moon. But she is not sublime; she seems simply a beautiful young girl who might have stepped from a Velázquez *bodegón.* The artist further breaks with tradition in his portrait of St. John *(above).* The saint,

usually depicted as an old man laboriously setting down scripture, is shown as a robust young figure contemplating his apocalyptic visions of the devil, in the guise of a three-headed dragon, and a mysterious winged woman.

Mother Doña Jerónima de la Fuente, 1620

The elegant austerity that graced the art of Velázquez from the beginning imbues the two paintings seen here. Mother Jerónima *(above)* was painted just before the 66-year-old nun left Seville to found a convent in the Philippines. The muted colors, the firm grip on the crucifix, and the determined stance and look underscore the nun's dedication. The absence of background and color intensifies the feeling of austerity; the crimson binding of the prayer book is the only flash of bright color Velázquez allowed himself. This same restraint dignifies his *Crucifixion (right).* The slack, pale figure seems to float on the Cross; He dies peacefully, as though asleep.

The Crucifixion, c. 1631-1632

Christ after the Flagellation Contemplated by the Christian Soul, 1626-1628

After Velázquez left Seville to spend the rest of his life at the court in Madrid, he painted a few more religious works. Among them were *The Crucifixion (preceding page)* and *Christ and the Christian Soul (above, detail at right)*. Both show his enduring commitment to realism. Above, Christ is portrayed as a muscular man of great presence. He is being adored by a child representing the soul, accompanied by a guardian angel. Despite the flogging that preceded His Crucifixion, Christ remains strong; His face and eyes, however, indicate His sorrow and understanding. Indeed, it is Christ's awareness and acceptance of His fate that give the painting both its compassion and its force.

The composition has a finely balanced tension; the rope that binds Christ leads to the stone column at the left while His head and body incline toward the figures at the right. Velázquez' quiet colors, painted over a red prime that shows through in places, add their special quality; blood from the whip lashes is the only vivid touch. So confident was the artist of his powers that he apparently executed this painting, as he did many of his works, without a single preliminary sketch.

III

The Royal Pleasures

Velázquez had every reason to be pleased with his decision to leave Seville and become a servant of the King. With his arrival at court he achieved the enviable position of being independent of commissions for a living. The emoluments and honors bestowed by Philip gave him a freedom from worry that no other Spanish artist of his day enjoyed. The assignments he received were all choice and usually spaced far enough apart to allow him to evaluate his artistic progress and gather strength and inspiration for the next challenge. The royal patronage was enlightened: both Philip and his First Minister, Olivares, were men of taste apparently unruffled by the painter's experiments in style. An artist with less inner strength might have lost drive in the face of such comfort and acceptance. If ever this happened to Velázquez in these early years it was never for long. He was a dedicated man, and a practical one. For someone of his background and aspirations, the court was the only place to be. For an artist of his talent, it was the only place in Spain where he could pursue the complete mastery of his craft.

On his return from Italy in 1631, he found the court in a jubilant mood. Although the economy remained as shaky as before, the birth in 1629 of Prince Baltasar Carlos *(left)* had lifted spirits and provided an excuse for the ostentatious display so beloved by the Spaniards. After eight years of waiting, there was at last a healthy male heir to the throne. For the baptism, a special corridor and staircase leading from the palace to the church were constructed and hung with tapestries. The baby was carried on the lap of the Countess of Olivares, wife of the Minister, who was herself borne on a sedan chair. Olivares marched alongside in a robe of silver, with sleeves dangling down to the ground, a peculiar getup that caused no end of comment among the courtiers following him. Throughout the baptism, the Countess sat like a queen on a "chair of rock crystal, the most costly piece of furniture ever seen in Europe." The Queen herself was not present at the ceremony; she was still recovering from the birth. The King, although restrained by custom from appearing, watched the baptism from a heavily draped pew. An orgy of celebrations followed. When the Queen regained sufficient strength to receive the tributes

Baltasar Carlos, heir to the throne, strikes a regal pose that belies his age in this portrait painted by Velázquez when the Prince was 16 months old. The boy's companion, one of the many dwarfs who served at court, holds a silver rattle and an apple.

Prince Baltasar Carlos with a Dwarf, 1631

King Philip had not allowed any other artist to paint him while Velázquez was in Italy. The painting above—known as the *Brown and Silver Philip* for its dominant color and elaborate ornamentation—was done soon after Velázquez' return and reveals the freer brush technique that was a product of the artist's Italian experience. This picture is one of only two royal portraits that Velázquez signed—the other is lost. The paper in Philip's hand *(detail)*, in the form of a petition, bears the artist's signature.

of her delighted subjects, the festivities broke out all over again. The bull-fights, parades and balls held in her honor went on for days, and the joyous King made his appearance at every one.

Philip had good reason to be pleased with himself—and more so than most people at the time could have known. Baltasar Carlos was only one of two sons he had fathered in 1629, and the other boy, like the Prince, was a healthy, handsome infant. In an age when children took sick easily and died, the King could thus consider himself doubly blessed.

His other son was illegitimate; he had been named Don Juan and taken to the Castle of Ocaña to be reared—a prince in waiting, as it were. Don Juan's mother was a famous actress, María Calderon, La Calderona, with whom Philip had been carrying on a protracted affair. The King seemed really in love with her and willing to continue the liaison, but in spite of his protests La Calderona broke off with him after the birth of Don Juan ended the last pretense of secrecy. She then did what was expected of her and entered a convent. Her fate exactly paralleled that of the other hapless women who suffered the misfortune of becoming mistresses to Philip: once the affair ended—either because Philip's ardor cooled or pregnancy led to public embarrassment—the woman had to withdraw from the world. No suitor could ever follow the King; this was the unwritten rule. The story goes that one girl at court became so upset by Philip's interest in her that she locked herself behind a door and cried out that she did not want to be a nun. The girl had good reason to be apprehensive: Philip is known to have produced at least 30 illegitimate offspring in his lifetime.

Secluded in the Castle of Ocaña, little Don Juan was never painted by Velázquez, but his half brother of course was. The artist had come back refreshed from his year-and-a-half stay in Italy, his vision enlarged by all that he had seen there. Into the picture of Baltasar Carlos he poured much of what he had taken in abroad, and the result is a painting of great richness. A similar richness pervades the portrait of the King that he painted shortly afterward—the so-called *Brown and Silver Philip* now in the London National Gallery. The King wears a handsome brown suit and black cape stitched all over with silver threads and ornaments. Gone is the old sobriety that obliged the artist to portray him entirely in black. As though in response to this dropping of restraints, Velázquez' brushstrokes became wonderfully free. The King's hair is long and lustrous, and he has grown a goatee and a mustache turned up at the ends. The transformation begun by Velázquez of Philip's features in 1624 is here complete: the King could almost be called handsome. But beyond conveying a hint of narcissism in Philip's nature, Velázquez did not play up the sensual aspects of the King's character—nor did he include any suggestion of his own feelings about the all-too-human behavior of a man who was supposed to be semidivine.

If Philip's love affairs were easily forgiven in a court that admired sexual swagger, his failure to be similarly aggressive in governmental affairs was another matter. Although now in his mid-twenties, he behaved after nearly 10 years on the throne as if he still considered himself too young for the task. Despite his acknowledged intelligence he continued to defer to Olivares in all matters of state. Even to himself he must have begun to appear a failure. He had the best of intentions but lacked the will to put them into effect. He mourned the plight of the oppressed people of Castile, who were taxed unmercifully to pay for the Thirty Years' War. "If my own lifeblood would remedy it," he once told his councilors, "I would cheerfully give it." But he let taxes go up. In gratitude for his recovery from his severe illness of 1627, he had vowed to redress wrongs in a six-point document spelling out reforms. Some small inequities for which he felt blame were corrected, but he failed to follow through and rectify much greater wrongs committed in his name by his ministers.

Rather than rule, Philip played. He found escape in an assortment of pleasures—not only love-making, but horseback riding, hunting and theatergoing. When conscience nagged, he drew the robes of state around him and threw himself into official ceremonial. Undoubtedly this helped convince him that he was doing his part, when in fact he was only performing a part. Philip was indeed a much better actor than king. But even this defense began to wear thin and as his feelings of uselessness grew, so did his despair. And with despair came guilt over what he considered to be his sinful behavior.

Paper work bored the young King—and yet this was the one duty he could not dodge. He might neglect to read important documents Olivares brought him, but he had to sign them. Apparently he let them pile up, and more than once he was admonished by Olivares for being dilatory. At one point, for example, the Minister bluntly told him in a note: "There is really no other course but that your Majesty should put your shoulder to the wheel." Olivares then threatened to quit. Philip's reply was in character: "I have resolved to do as you ask me, for the sake of God, of myself, and of you. I return you this paper with this reply, so that you may make it an heirloom of your house, that your descendants may learn how to speak to kings in matters that touch their fame, and that they may know what an ancestor they had. I should like to leave it in my archives to teach my children, and other kings, how they should submit to what is just and proper—I, THE KING." Like so many of Philip's resolutions, this one was short-lived; it only reinforced his dependence upon his Minister by convincing him that he was unfit to be king.

Philip and Olivares were opposites. Olivares was strong, resourceful, energetic, disciplined, dedicated. He could also be overweening and ruthless. Philip was weak, lazy and totally undisciplined. In his position of power, Olivares preyed upon Philip's weaknesses, and Philip let him.

The King's diffidence had its roots in his upbringing. From the start, much more had been expected of him than he could ever fulfill. Baptized Philip Dominic after St. Dominic, the firebrand founder of the Holy Inquisition, he had been allotted the task of carrying on the saint's merciless war against heresy. He was to grow up without questioning this mission, even though he was temperamentally unsuited for it.

Philip's mother died when he was six. His father, Philip III, paid him little attention, and he was raised by women and educated by churchmen who tried to make of his childhood a round of devotions and study—apparently with little success. At an early age Philip acquired a love for the theater and as a boy performed often in the masques and plays given at the court. At nine he showed the aplomb of a veteran actor. Playing Cupid, he came on stage in a swaying chariot. The motion made him queasy, and when he stepped down and advanced toward the audience, he vomited. But he and the show went on, and as a courtier noted later, the Prince "performed his part very prettily."

Any chance Philip may have had of developing some independence was dashed when Olivares appeared, ready to mold the boy according to his own ambitious ends. Olivares came from an old family. He had been destined for a career in the Church when the death of his older brother suddenly thrust upon him the role of head of the family. He set his sights high, and his connections soon won him an important position. He entered the life of the Prince, then 11, as Gentleman of the Bedchamber, a post that enabled him to take over complete management of the princely household—and the boy with it. Philip's marriage to Isabel, the daughter of Henry IV of France and Marie de' Medici, did not lessen Olivares' influence. He began to impress upon Philip what together they might do for Spain, and he found a listener, a youth in the expanding phase of idealism for whom all change seemed possible.

As Olivares' influence grew, Philip received little guidance from his father. Philip III was a complete weakling who lived for pomp and ceremony alone. When told in 1619 that Spain was "being totally ruined and exhausted," that his people were fleeing abroad to escape taxation, and that something had to be done about it, and quickly, Philip III broke down and sank into a depression from which he never recovered. As he lay dying late in the winter of 1621 in a room piled high with the dried and withered remains of saints brought in to comfort him, he called for his young heir, "that you might see how it all ends." It ended horribly, with the old King clutching in panic the same crucifix that his father and grandfather had clasped in their final moments. "A fine account we shall give to God of our government" were among his last, despairing words.

Thus, when Philip came to the throne at 16, he stood so much in need of his mentor Olivares that he made him his most trusted adviser. As "the favorite," Olivares continued to dictate the pattern of Philip's life. It was he who introduced Philip to the dissolute pleasures of Madrid and was unmoved when the King's former tutor, the Archbishop of Granada, complained: "People are gossiping about it all over Madrid, and things are being said about it which add little to the Sovereign's credit or dignity." Olivares shrugged off the criticism: "The King is sixteen, and he [Olivares refers to himself in the third person] is thirty-four, and it is not to be expected that they are to be kept in ignorance of what is going on in the world. It is good that the King should see all phases of life, bad as well as good. Besides, he never trusts the King with anyone else."

And indeed Olivares never trusted the King with anyone else. He was the last to leave Philip's bedroom at night and the first to enter it in the morning. He would open the window, pull back the draperies around the bed and then launch the day's business. How Philip, with his eyes not yet fully open, must have cowered in the bed sheets at the sight of Oli-

Intermarriage has long been one of the favorite ploys of royalty to assuage rivalries and forge alliances, and the Habsburgs were among its foremost practitioners. The engraving above shows a double wedding between archrivals France and Spain that was arranged in 1615. At the left, France's Queen Marie de' Medici offers her son, the future King Louis XIII, and his sister Isabel to the children of Philip III of Spain, Anne and the future Philip IV. At the time Louis and Anne were both 14; Philip was 10 and Isabel 13. Not surprisingly, the children closely resemble one another, a result of their common Habsburg lineage.

vares looming there. And what a terrifying figure Olivares was. In time he took to the intimidating practice of stuffing his pockets with documents, shoving them rolled up under his arms and sticking them into his hatband. His enemies began to call him "the bogeyman" or "bugaboo of kings"—behind his back.

Philip was not the only person intimidated by Olivares. His gruff manner would have been enough to put most people off, but he combined it with a capacity for work that left even the most diligent secretaries worn out and drove four prematurely to their graves. His day unfolded according to an exhausting schedule. He rose at 5, received his confessor and granted audiences. Between 9 and 11 he went over reports with his secretaries; at 11 he held more audiences. Then, after a bite to eat, he settled down again to business and worked on until 11 at night with only a short pause for dinner. Never did he seem to waste a moment. "From his bedchamber to his study, from his study to his coach, out strolling, in the odd corner, on the stairs," wrote a contemporary, "he would hear and dispatch an infinite number of people."

As his power increased, Olivares grew more and more jealous of it. Blindly confident of his own abilities, he rebuffed criticism with violent anger. His way became the only way. To keep the King from any influence but his own, he progressively isolated Philip. He kept watch over the King's two brothers, Carlos and Fernando, and parried their moves toward him. He helped sow dissension between Philip and the Queen by supplying him with mistresses, usually actresses.

The Queen reacted to the King's dissipations with disgust, but she was apparently more concerned with other matters. She loved pleasure as much as her husband did, and could be manipulated almost as easily. In some ways she was the perfect leading lady for Philip. Her gay, although at times irascible, spirit brought new life to the court, and she shared Philip's love of the theater. She was, however, jaded beyond her years, and novel amusements had continually to be devised for her. Some of these were strange indeed. Fights would be deliberately started between unsuspecting women so that the Queen might watch them brawl from some hidden vantage point. Her greatest pleasure, it was said, was to observe from behind a screen the panic created in a theater when snakes were released upon the floor. Even in the dissolute 17th Century Spanish court this was considered eccentric.

As time wore on, Olivares seemed increasingly reluctant to share with the King the details of government. His job was a difficult one, and no doubt he had to discourage interference from the inexperienced Philip. Gradually he began reducing his visits to the royal apartment from three a day to one, and that one to a brief 15 minutes. In fact self-protection made it increasingly necessary to keep the King in the dark. Olivares' policies were proving disastrous. Spain's commitment of men and money to the Catholic cause in the Thirty Years' War had brought her no real gain. After Protestant Sweden's entry into the war under the powerful leadership of King Gustavus Adolphus, Spain and her Austrian ally met two shattering defeats—one at the Battle of Breitenfeld in 1631 and the other a year later at Lützen. Moreover, Spain's continued presence in Central Europe on the side of Austria aggravated France, and war with that nation, too, now seemed imminent. At home the problem was still money—money to support the old war, money to prepare for the new one. Tax after tax was levied on the people of Castile. For further contributions Olivares turned once more to Catalonia but his pressures on the Catalans did little more than deepen their resistance to his mutual defense plan, the Union of Arms, through which he still hoped to achieve Spanish unity. And when he attempted to impose a tax on salt in the fiercely independent Basque provinces, he kindled the first flames of insurrection within the Iberian peninsula. The Basques refused to pay. Olivares threatened to send 30,000 troops to force them to comply. "We will await their coming with 3,000 and beat them," was the answer. The salt tax was never collected.

As discontent with his policies grew, Olivares found it more expedient than ever to distract and please the King—and to do so, he dug deeply into his own purse. In his wife he had a willing helpmeet who could always be depended upon to come up with entertainment to enchant the King and Queen. But on June 1, 1631, the Countess so outdid herself with a party at her brother's estate that her husband felt constrained to give an even more magnificent one in his own name. All things were possible to Olivares, and he did not hesitate to set the date for his fete three weeks after his wife's. He attended to many details himself, "determined," an observer wrote, "to show the extreme love and care with which he serves our Lord the King, and how easily he conquers the most difficult tasks by means of it."

Again the grounds of the Countess' brother were used, as well as those adjacent. An open-air theater was built and several little garden houses were made of flowers and leaves. Stands were erected for six orchestras and choirs, and three leading literary figures were ordered to create two plays, which by some miracle turned out to be well written and charming, although one was composed in a day and the other over the course of three days. At 9 o'clock the guests began arriving, to be presented at the entrance with gifts of perfume, bouquets and handkerchiefs. The ladies were also presented with little vessels of red clay infused with scent. Inexplicably, it had become social custom for ladies not only to sip water from these vessels but to bite off and chew small bits of the unglazed clay. (Such a little crock is being offered to the Princess in *Las Meninas, page 178*.) After the first play, *Who Lies Most Thrives Most*, the royal party adjourned to the garden houses and changed into disguises "strange in shape and fashion," which they wore to the performance of the second play, *The Night of St. John*. At midnight they strolled to another bower for dinner, personally served by Olivares and his countess. And not until dawn did they go home.

The lavishness of the party was just a taste of things to come. Olivares had already launched a project that Spain could ill afford but that he knew would delight the King. He had begun construction of a grand new palace. The existing royal residence, the Alcázar, had originally been a medieval castle and, despite extensive remodeling, including the addition of an impressive façade in the 16th Century, it remained a

In a rare gibe at Philip IV, a political satirist based his cartoon on the most popular piece of literature of the day, Miguel de Cervantes' picaresque novel *Don Quixote de la Mancha*, the adventures of an aging knight and his faithful squire, Sancho Panza. The cartoon, which surreptitiously appeared in 1641, shows Philip as Don Quixote and his First Minister, Olivares, as Sancho. This dangerous satire—men were jailed for less —equates Philip's costly and futile wars with Quixote's windmill-tilting crusades.

forbidding structure. It contained 500 rooms but these were either so cramped or so dark that an amazed Italian visitor wrote home to say there was not a single good room in the whole edifice. Nearly 1,000 people, many of them soldiers, lived at the Alcázar, and it was Philip's responsibility to provide for all. He spent at least a million escudos a year to keep his ménage going—candles alone cost 60,000 ducats, 600 times the price he paid Velázquez for the large painting, *Bacchus*. Never was the need for economy greater than now as war with France drew closer; yet Olivares went boldly ahead with the new palace.

A site was chosen on the other side of Madrid from the Alcázar, and several hundred acres were appropriated for the grounds (the present Retiro Park is part of the original plot). Clearing of the land began almost immediately, and for a while people thought that all Olivares had in mind was a modest retreat of some sort. But as construction got underway on the main building in 1630, the enormous scope of the project became apparent: there were to be a theater, a plaza, game preserves, and a wooded park complete with lakes, grottoes and cascades. By October 1632 work was well enough along for an inaugural ceremony to be held, and at this Olivares turned over to the King the gold keys to the Buen Retiro—the Good Retreat, as the palace came to be called. But Philip's delight in his prospective new home was tempered by events: shortly before the inaugural ceremony he had had to accompany Olivares to Barcelona, there personally to entreat the Catalans to support the Crown in its ventures in Europe. But the response Philip evoked was lukewarm and the atmosphere openly hostile to him and Olivares. Soon thereafter his younger brother, Carlos, died, adding personal grief to diplomatic disappointment.

Now more than ever it must have seemed crucial to Olivares to finish the Buen Retiro. To distract the depressed monarch, and to impress others with the power of Castile, he rushed the palace to completion. One thousand workers labored day and night to have it ready for its opening in 1634. The English Ambassador, taking note of the frenzied building activity, found himself wondering "what will happen when the palace is burdened with such a posse of people as usually resort to such pastimes, the mortar being yet greene." Despite its supposedly weak foundations, the Buen Retiro withstood the onslaught; the housewarming went on for four days, "much to their Majesties' contentment." Again Philip had been diverted. But the palace was already a sore subject among many Madrileños. The people "suffer it worse," wrote the English Ambassador, "because they say it is a fancy of [Olivares], and they deeply resented the taxes that he continued to impose upon their wine, meat and oil to help pay for it."

Built around several courtyards, the Buen Retiro contained numerous well-lighted rooms filled with precious objects. Those who complained about the great cost of the palace could only approve of the way it had been furnished. What had not come from the other royal palaces had been pried from the rich by Olivares as "donations." Even Olivares' brother-in-law, the Count of Monterrey, was obliged to turn over the greater part of the art collection he had amassed while a diplomat in Italy.

Velázquez must have been well aware of the highhandedness of Oli-

Perhaps the most famous Spanish royal jewel is the huge pearl worn by Queen Isabel, first wife of Philip IV, in the equestrian portrait Velázquez painted for the Hall of Realms *(detail at top)*. It is shown actual size in the photograph above. As the story goes, the bell-shaped pearl was found by a slave in a Gulf of Panama oyster so small that it was almost thrown away. It arrived in Spain in 1554 and Philip II gave it to his betrothed, Mary Tudor of England, but after her death it was returned to Spain and worn by successive queens until 1813, when it was carried away to France in the booty that Joseph Bonaparte collected. Nicknamed "La Peregrina" (The Wanderer) for its extraordinary travels, the gem was bought in 1969 by the actor Richard Burton, for his wife, Elizabeth Taylor.

vares, the weakness of the King, the sham of the new palace, the sad state of Spanish affairs. And yet he seems not to have been demoralized. He was to do some of his finest work for the Buen Retiro. Something beyond duty, something stronger than reputation, seems to have motivated him, and this no doubt was his sense of honor. Velázquez was in the truest sense of the word a nobleman, and the quality he valued most was the one he so often got into his pictures of people, whether of poor *bodegón* types or of the King—dignity. Philip's ability to set his face into a mask, behind which he hid the pain of his guilt, did not go unnoticed, or unadmired, by the artist.

As the greatest painter in the court, it fell to Velázquez to help uphold the dignity of the monarchy, and in his assignment for the Buen Retiro he faced the greatest challenge of his career. He was to provide five portraits of the royal family for a grand salon to be called the Hall of Realms. This had been conceived as a showcase of Philip's reign, and in addition to the royal likenesses it was to include 12 military scenes celebrating victories won in the King's name and 10 paintings showing the labors of Hercules. It would have been impossible for Velázquez to paint all of these, but he did reserve for himself one of the military scenes, and he seems to have been responsible for coordinating the decorative scheme as well. Among the other artists supplying pictures for the Hall were his two old rivals, Carducho and Caxés, and one of the judges of the competition that had seen him pitted against them, Maino.

Velázquez was fortunate in having several assistants to help him with the project, and among them may have been a capable young man called Juan Bautista Martínez del Mazo. Eventually Mazo learned to mimic Velázquez' style so well that it is almost impossible to tell, in some paintings, where one left off and the other began. Theirs was a good relationship, not unlike that between Velázquez and his teacher Pacheco, and history in a sense repeated itself when Velázquez gave his only surviving child, his daughter Francisca, to Mazo in marriage in 1633. Everything about the wedding was as it should be: the King and Olivares served as the couple's sponsors, and later Velázquez arranged to have his own title of Usher of the Chamber transferred to his son-in-law, thus assuring the young man of a respectable position at court.

This must have been a particularly satisfying time for Velázquez. In his career and in his personal life he was blessed. And he had not ceased to advance in the hierarchy of the court. For a hidalgo like him, this would have been of paramount importance, since a man's nobility was measured here not just by the purity of his blood or the grace of his manner, but by his rank. Velázquez seems to have been every bit as concerned with status as he was with his reputation as an artist. When he was made Gentleman of the Wardrobe in 1634, a courtier remarked that the painter must be aiming at the higher rank of Gentleman of the Bedchamber, a position he was indeed to achieve nine years later.

The speed with which everything connected with the Buen Retiro had to be done doubtless put the artist under great pressure. He had to finish his paintings in time for the opening of the Hall of Realms in April 1635. Rather than paint entirely new portraits of Philip's parents and the Queen, he reverted to three that he is believed to have begun before going to Italy and left for someone else to finish. He freshened these up, repainting some areas and relieving the stiffness of the compositions with free and lucid strokes. He devoted special attention to the likeness of the Queen. Isabel hated posing and she apparently refused to sit for Velázquez at this time. It would be interesting to know how she felt about him; he was, after all, the protégé of Olivares, whom she despised. To bring her portrait up to date Velázquez was obliged to fall back on another recent portrait of her. She was an attractive woman, but here she sits upon her horse tight-lipped, inscrutable, the prisoner of her voluminous robes *(page 75)*.

Whatever time was thus saved the artist applied to the execution of his masterpieces for the Hall of Realms—an enormous picture of Philip mounted on a chestnut horse *(page 76)*, a smaller one of Baltasar Carlos astride a spirited pony *(page 79)*, and *The Surrender of Breda (pages 80-83)*. All three were painted with the big, bold brushstrokes of a man fully in command of his powers. While depicting majesty, the portraits are in themselves majestic—works of verve and strength, unburdened by the cherubim and angels other artists of Velázquez' day included to set royalty apart from mere mortals. Their regal impact derives from the erect carriage of Philip and Baltasar Carlos, the thrust of their magnificent steeds, and the sweeping views of the snow-capped Guadarrama Mountains. Landscape was practically a new concern for Velázquez, and yet here he demonstrated how well he understood the modifying effects of atmosphere on objects in the open air. He gave to both portraits the blue-green-and-grayish tones of an overcast day, which mute the pinks of the flying sashes and bring all the other colors into harmonious play. Interestingly, in a country of sunshine, Velázquez ignored the blazing light of Castile, and kept to the tonality of a world under the shadow of clouds.

The portraits show Velázquez once more in his role as court painter —taciturn, with no comment to make on his sitters. *The Surrender of Breda*, however, reveals that he did have something to say and could say it with force. Ostensibly the painting is the celebration of a great victory —but it is actually much more, an eloquent statement about honor addressed to the Spanish conscience. Breda was a supposedly impregnable fortress town in the Netherlands controlling the roads to Utrecht and Amsterdam. Its strategic location, plus the fact that the Dutch launched raids from it into Spanish Flanders, had led Philip to order his ablest general, Ambrosio Spínola, to attack it in 1624. Spínola was a brilliant engineer and had miles-long trenches dug to flood and cut off the city. But in his Dutch foe, Justin of Nassau, he found his match, and soon all Europe was watching what was not only a test of power between Catholic Spain and Protestant Holland, but a battle of wits between two great generals. Observers arrived from as far away as Poland to study the moves and countermoves of the besiegers and the besieged. The Dutch held out 11 months, capitulating only after a relief effort had failed and their food and ammunition had given out.

Then Spínola made an unheard-of gesture. His troops expected him to impose harsh terms on the vanquished. But his admiration for the brav-

Chief among the decorations awarded by the Habsburg monarchs was the Order of the Golden Fleece, an emblem worn by Philip IV in nearly all of his portraits by Velázquez. The dangling insignia, shown enlarged in the detail at center above, represents the golden ram that the Greek hero Jason won in the Argonaut legend; it can also be seen hanging at the bottom in the overall view of the heavy gold collar whose links symbolize flints and fire-steels. The Order, founded in 1430, was awarded at first only to Roman Catholics of aristocratic birth; its purpose was to promote the chivalric ideal. It still exists among international nobility: 20th Century holders are kings of Belgium and Greece and the Duke of Windsor.

ery and resourcefulness of his foes was so great that he granted amnesty to the citizens of Breda, allowing them to evacuate the city with their colors and weapons intact. Eyewitnesses report that he waited on horseback for the Dutch commander to emerge from the city. As Justin approached, Spínola saluted him. The Dutch reacted with "composed countenances and voices," and dipped their banners. The men met, and Spínola is supposed to have addressed words of encouragement to Justin and arranged an honor guard for him. This is the moment painted by Velázquez. While the Dutch and Spanish staffs stand off to either side, Spínola in black armor extends his arm to Justin in welcome, gently touching him on the back. Velázquez made Spínola a figure of great compassion. All Spínola's magnanimity is compressed into the single gesture of his outstretched arm, bridging the gap between two enemies, and the gesture is all the more moving for the response it produces in the tired Dutchman, who extends the key to the city to him. There is a look of unutterable sorrow in Justin's face.

The news of Spain's victory reached Madrid 10 days after the surrender and Olivares boasted with characteristic exaggeration that "our victory was won against the forces of the entire world." But ultimately what captured people's imaginations was not so much the victory, which in a few years' time proved of small import, but Spínola's chivalric behavior. He became a symbol of honor. The playwright Calderón de la Barca re-created the siege on the stage, and in the last scene of his play had Spínola say to Justin: "The valor of the conquered makes the conqueror famous." Spínola could almost be saying that in Velázquez' painting. We know that Velázquez saw this play, or at least knew of it, for he borrowed something from it that is not mentioned in any of the descriptions of the actual event: the handing over of the key.

Velázquez painted *The Surrender of Breda* almost 10 years after the victory. Much had happened in the interim. There was a need now to look back upon past triumphs, to find consolation in them. And there was need for honor. Nothing illustrates this better than the fate that befell Spínola. After diligently upholding the Spanish cause in Flanders for many years, he had been called back to Madrid in 1628. There he urged that a truce be signed with the Dutch, pointing out that decades of war had failed to bring victory. He felt that such a truce would enable Spain to improve its commerce and stabilize its finances. Olivares would hear nothing of it: war was the only answer. Despite Olivares' open hostility, Spínola continued to state his case. For a while it looked as though he might be making headway. The painter and diplomat Rubens, who knew both Spínola and Olivares, said of the general's situation at the court, "I am afraid that this favor will last only as long as he remains there, but will change as easily to envy and jealousy as soon as he has turned his back."

Rubens proved right. Spínola was soon ordered to a command in northern Italy. He waged a brilliant campaign in Mantua and had surrounded the key fortress of Casale when his men came down with plague. His pleas for reinforcements went unheard. When he asked for permission to negotiate a settlement that would still have been to Spain's advantage, he learned that Olivares had withdrawn his peacemaking credentials. He had no option but to retreat. He died soon thereafter, a broken man who on his deathbed kept repeating the words "honor" and "reputation."

It is curious that Velázquez should have gone out of his way to make of a man who was the victim of his patron Olivares a figure of such great sympathy. Still, he threw himself with zeal into the execution of the canvas, the biggest and most complex work of his entire career. Painting *The Surrender of Breda* posed enormous technical problems, and the way Velázquez solved them is proof of the richness of his imagination and his devotion to the subject. By now both Spínola and Justin were dead. Yet as famous men they had to be rendered with great verisimilitude. This was all the more crucial in the case of Spínola, who had been well known at court. Velázquez was fortunate in that he had traveled with the general to Italy in 1629; he could fall back on his recollection. But he must have been hard-pressed to come up with a lifelike image of Justin when only engraved portraits were available. Even more challenging was the landscape background. Velázquez had never been to the Netherlands. He probably consulted Dutch and French engravings of Breda and its surroundings for topographical details. The miracle is how close he came to reproducing the actual environment. Even the light with which he bathed the scene is the cool, blue light of the Netherlands.

But then everything about *The Surrender of Breda* is real, alive. To see how dynamic a painting it is, it need only be compared with the other surviving military scenes for the Hall of Realms. They are stiff tableaux, acted by not very good players. Velázquez' painting is a drama, filled with motion. Men and horses jostle each other, faces turn right and left and look straight out of the picture—and yet not one gesture, not one glance detracts from the encounter between Spínola and Justin in the middle foreground.

The painting is marvelously unified. Placing the Spaniards on the right and the Dutch on the left was a relatively simple compositional device, parentheses around the main action; yet Velázquez manipulated it in such a way that it seems anything but simple. He depicted the Dutch full length, and the Spaniards half length, cut off by the bulk of Spínola's restless horse. Further to vary this arrangement, he gave each man a different pose and each a different expression. Twenty-eight upright lances in the upper right background serve as a kind of bold punctuation, interrupting the movements of the men and horses, and connecting the top and bottom halves of the painting. Color contributes its own unity: although brown predominates, blue, pink and green ripple across the canvas. And again, as in the portraits of the King and Prince, atmosphere, the mist over land and sky, modulates the various hues and encloses the painting in its own envelope of light and air.

In *The Surrender of Breda* Velázquez was no longer concerned with the way things looked, as he had been in his Seville years, but with the way they seemed. Thus he did not concentrate on details here as he did in the *bodegones*: lace, satin, plumes all lapse into a haze of brushstrokes upon close examination—and paint itself becomes something to appreciate and enjoy. Velázquez had begun to see the world in a whole new way —a wholly personal way.

Peasants, Gods and Heroes

Life as a court painter could have been a stifling trap for Velázquez. It was not an easy role to play; an artist's urge for self-expression had constantly to be measured against the necessity of pleasing high-placed patrons. Throughout history, lesser painters have pandered to royalty in return for the bounties of court life. Velázquez liked the life, and as court painter he worked diligently to build the image of Spain. He gave his kings and queens majesty, his leaders nobility and power. But Velázquez was also honest, and too talented to restrict himself to routine, sycophantic performances. Even portraits that flattered are full of insights.

Fortunately, Velázquez' two most important patrons —Philip IV and his First Minister, Olivares—had the taste and sensibility to recognize and encourage brilliance when they saw it. Velázquez remained notably free of interference. He was able to undertake original work, peopling animated scenes from mythology with expressive 17th Century Spaniards *(right)*, rather than with stiff renditions of stylized gods in Olympian costumes. As one reward for his achievements, the King granted his painter a trip to Italy. The paintings Velázquez produced during his stay there bore out the promise of his work at court, reflecting a new command of color and space. The experience in Italy stood Velázquez in good stead when he returned to the Madrid court, where he undertook even more difficult work.

A grinning ruffian of a Spaniard, holding a bowl of cheer, served Velázquez as a model for a disciple of the wine god in *Bacchus (following pages)*. Here the artist reveals a mood of high humor; his happy rogue is infected with the joyous spirit with which Spaniards traditionally embrace a fiesta.

Detail from
Bacchus

138

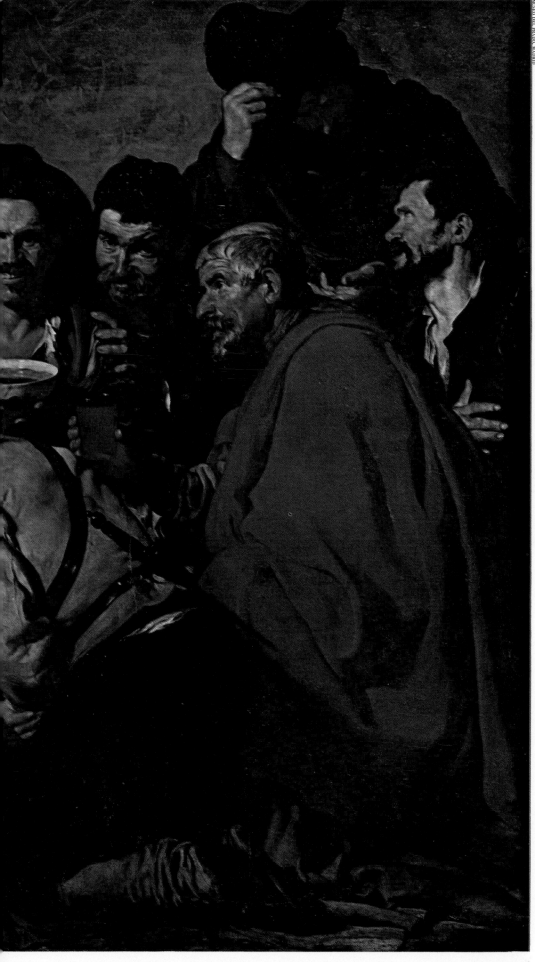

Bacchus, 1628

This lively scene of Bacchus, the Greek god of wine, and his convivial followers was one of Velázquez' early works in Madrid. Its irreverent tone reveals the freedom he felt to deviate from the respectful treatment traditionally given mythological subjects; some details suggest he may also have intended to comment on the present. Ostensibly the painting shows a sleek and sassy young Bacchus as he places a garland on the head of a kneeling drinker while other rascals cluster about.

Yet for all this mythic festivity, Velázquez' subjects are shown with a seedy quality. The artist may have had in mind public drinking spectacles: on such occasions peasants would be plied with wine until they were sodden —largely to amuse an audience of courtiers. But Velázquez also adds a reminder of Spain's poverty. In the background a beggar humbly tips his hat and extends his hand for alms. This symbol of charity acts as a counterpoint to the drunkards who follow the false god of fable. Velázquez has blurred his features suggestively, however, to emphasize his place in the background of the scene.

The Forge of Vulcan, 1630

Many a young painter has found that a trip to Italy has a liberating effect on his art; Velázquez was no exception. Studying the works of such masters as Tintoretto and Titian, he not only made his colors more subtle but learned how to use the play of light to suggest the three-dimensional spacing of figures. His success with these new techniques may be seen in *The Forge of Vulcan (above, detail right),* which he completed in Rome in 1630.

In the painting the Roman sun god Apollo is telling Vulcan, god of fire and metalwork, that he has seen Vulcan's wife, Venus, committing adultery with Mars,

god of war. The news evokes shocked reactions, ranging from the growing rage in Vulcan's eyes to the openmouthed astonishment of the worker at the right. As in *Bacchus,* a hint of humor is apparent in the work. The baby face and admonishing finger of Apollo make him seem more a schoolboy tattletale than a powerful sun god, while the cuckolded Vulcan and his crew seem a group of common Spanish laborers out of an early Velázquez *bodegón*—elements of which the artist retains here in the finely detailed still lifes of the armor, the tools near the anvil and the white vase on the shelf above the hearth.

Philip III, Equestrian, 1634-1635

Queen Isabel of Bourbon, Equestrian, 1634-1635

Velázquez returned from Italy in 1631 to find that construction had begun on Philip IV's new palace, the Buen Retiro. The artist was quickly pressed into service to help decorate a cavernous room called the Hall of Realms. Apparently the two paintings shown here had been started before Velázquez' Italian trip; they were finished by other, less skillful hands in a stiff and formal style. On his return to Madrid Velázquez set out to enliven them. Evidently he wanted to do so without detracting from their impressiveness—they are about 12 by 12 feet. (They were widened by having canvas strips added to their sides, possibly to accommodate them to their new location.)

Velázquez completely repainted the face of Philip IV's queen, Isabel of Bourbon, working from his earlier pictures of her because she hated to pose. He did not retouch the Queen's robe, which is ornamented with her initials, "IB," repeated hundreds of times; but he probably added the ample forelock to the horse's head and moved the position of its raised left front leg.

In the equestrian portrait of Philip IV's father, Philip III, Velázquez' retouching of the horse's head was more elaborate *(detail, far left)*. He gave the animal a flowing mane and forelock tumbling around an ornate gold bridle. The added mane covered the original reins, their outlines disappearing under the cascade of curly hair.

Philip IV, Equestrian, 1634-1635

As an image builder, Velázquez was unsurpassed. In paintings like these two equestrian portraits, he made King Philip IV *(above)* and First Minister Olivares *(right)* seem to be all-powerful leaders. Showing them on horseback helped. In 17th Century Spain all men of rank were skilled horsemen, but Philip was reputedly the finest rider in the land, and Olivares was a close second. Cynics might find it hard to believe that either was quite that proficient, but in Velázquez' painting the King unquestionably knows what he is about. Erect in the saddle, he is plainly master of his mount, if not of his realm. Here, as always, he has the bearing of majesty.

The portrait of Olivares, probably executed about the same time as the King's, also conveys a sense of power and command. A thick-set, round-shouldered man who tended to fatness, Olivares is shown to good advantage; his half-turned position disguises his portliness. Everything about the portrait suggests action—Olivares points his baton, his horse rears, smoke rises from a battlefield in the background. Those touches were all part of the image. Olivares, while commander in chief of the King's armies, never set foot on an actual battlefield.

Don Gaspar de Guzmán, Conde de Olivares, Duque de San Lúcar la Mayor, Equestrian, 1634-1635-

Prince Baltasar Carlos, Equestrian, 1634-1635

Velázquez had a special technical problem in executing this portrait of young Prince Baltasar Carlos. The painting was intended to hang high over a doorway in the Hall of Realms, and the artist had to take this into account in depicting the Prince's pony. When the painting is seen head on, the pony's belly appears bloated; when seen from below, the rider and mount seem less distorted (as can be noted by tilting this book away from the eyes at an angle of approximately 45°). The Prince, aged four or five at the time he sat for the portrait, exudes confidence as he grasps the reins and sits manfully in the saddle, his pink sash trailing in the wind. The artist gained his effects here through great economy of paint and a hazy definition of features, techniques acquired in Italy and quite different from those he had used before. In the detail at left the paint is magically thin; the eyes seem mere dots and the nose an indistinct blob. Even the shadow of the hat that crosses the Prince's brow is but a suggestion.

The Surrender of Breda, 1634-1635

Ondersteunen ne of the 12 scenes of great Spanish battles that decorated the Hall of Realms was Velázquez' depiction of the celebrated surrender of Breda. Breda was a well-fortified town in the Netherlands that fell to a Spanish siege in 1624, ten years before Velázquez memorialized the event. Dutch resistance to the Spanish forces had been heroic and the conquering general, Ambrosio Spínola, instead of sacking the town and punishing the defenders, treated them with dignity. In this massive 12-foot-wide painting, Velázquez caught the moment when the worn and defeated Dutch general, Justin of Nassau, presents Spínola with the key to Breda. At the same time, the Spaniard consoles the loser with a gesture that seems to represent the epitome of Spanish honor and noblesse.

The scene is complex, a mixture of motion and stopped action. In the background the besieged city and battlefield smolder and smoke as the recently contending forces gather to witness the surrender. The faces of the Spanish officers behind Spínola reflect pity for the vanquished and pride in themselves; the erect lances of their soldiers convey the sense of a battle well fought by well-trained troops. Spínola's horse, restlessly moving among the men, adds to the immediacy of the scene. (The stallion that served as the model was the favorite mount of Philip IV. It also appears among the Dutch at left, and is the same animal that Philip is riding on page 76.)

The Dutch soldiers, exhausted after the 11-month-long siege, seem less animated than the Spaniards. But they present a tableau of real men perfectly captured in an instant *(detail, overleaf)*. The young noble in the white tunic is painted in an impressionistic way, his features blurred, perhaps to create a sense of depth and certainly to add to the sense of spontaneous movement and life. Clearly, the painter was pleased with the monumental work. He provided himself with a place to sign it—the piece of paper in the lower right foreground—but, inexplicably, never did affix his signature.

84

IV

An Age
of Giants

About the time Velázquez was
born, the Italian-trained artist
known as El Greco, then in his
early fifties, executed the brooding
landscape at left, a view of El
Greco's adopted Toledo and the
River Tagus that winds beneath
its hillside. In this vast green-gray
world of rocky terrain and rolling
clouds, human beings are only
insignificant black dots on the
bridge *(left center)* and pinpoints of
white in the river and along its
banks *(lower right)*. Ostensibly
only a landscape, *View of Toledo* is
actually a powerful, foreboding
commentary on the inadequacy of
man in the face of God's works.

El Greco: *View of Toledo*,
c. 1595-1600

Regarded solely from a cultural standpoint, the 44-year reign of Philip
IV could be called a golden age. During the 17th Century, Spanish theater, poetry and painting came into full flower, and the King himself had
much to do with this. His need for constant diversion helped make him
one of the greatest patrons of the arts Spain has known. He commanded
the services not only of Velázquez but of some of the giants of Spanish literature, including the poets Luis de Góngora y Argote and Francisco de
Quevedo y Villegas and the playwrights Lope de Vega and Calderón de
la Barca. The King's appetite for plays, in particular, was insatiable; even
the prolific Lope de Vega, who wrote at least 1,500 dramas in his lifetime, must have been hard-pressed at times to keep up with the royal demand. During the winter of 1622 and 1623, when Philip was osten-
tatiously tightening purse strings and reforming his official household,
no fewer than 43 new plays were performed for him and the Queen.

Philip's patronage reached its peak with the construction and decoration of the Buen Retiro. Nine leading artists, in addition to Velázquez,
provided paintings for its Hall of Realms alone. At the opening of the palace one of the most magnificent theatrical spectacles ever presented was
staged on a barge floating on the *estanque,* an enormous pond in the gardens. It was a musical by Calderón commissioned for the occasion and
based on the Greek myth of Ulysses and the enchantress Circe. The special effects included a shipwreck and the demolition of Circe's palace as ar-
tillery and fireworks boomed away. The King and his retinue watched
from gondolas, and were so taken with the production that Philip made
Calderón a knight of the Order of Santiago.

Along with Philip, the great benefactor of the arts in 17th Century
Spain was the Church—or rather, the many churches and religious houses scattered throughout the realm (there were 9,000 monasteries in Castile
alone). In the long run they did more to give shape and direction to Spanish art, if not to Spanish literature, than the Crown. Indeed, to many people the term "Spanish painting" automatically conjures up the names of
El Greco, Ribera, Zurbarán and Murillo—and the memory of museums
and cathedrals all over Spain filled with their pictures of saints and their

scenes of the Holy Family and of Christ's Passion. While Velázquez' talent bloomed in the secular soil of the court, the talents of these other painters were nourished in the abiding faith of the Spanish people.

El Greco, the greatest of Spain's religious painters, was not strictly a contemporary of Velázquez'—their lives overlapped by only 15 years —nor did the older man exert any detectable influence on Velázquez. But Spanish painting as we think of it today began with El Greco. Ironically, he was not a Spaniard, but a foreigner of Greek ancestry who came to Spain when he was past 30. The name by which he is commonly known means "The Greek"; his real name, which he invariably signed in Greek letters on his canvas, was Domenikos Theotokopoulos. He was born on the island of Crete, then a Venetian possession, in 1541. Although he may have received some formal training in his homeland, his real artistic education took place in Venice, where he moved sometime before he was 20. There he spent several years in the workshop of Titian, acquiring a style basically Venetian. Even when he entered upon his expressionistic phase later in life, he continued in the Venetian mode, placing primary emphasis on color and light and, from these, building form.

Early in the 1570s, El Greco went to Rome in hope of making a name for himself. He was lucky to secure the backing of Giulio Clovio, a painter who enjoyed the patronage of the powerful Cardinal Alessandro Farnese. Clovio seems to have gotten him lodgings in the cardinal's palace, and there El Greco was befriended by the cardinal's librarian, Fulvio Orsini, a patrician and great humanist. Despite their help, he did not flourish in Rome, perhaps because he was a painter of the Venetian school in a city of Michelangelo's followers. According to an early biographer, he shocked his fellow artists by saying that if Michelangelo's *Last Judgment* —which was then under fire for its nudity—were destroyed, he would replace it with a painting of his own, distinguished by "honesty and decorum." The Roman artists supposedly became so angry at El Greco's presumption that he had to flee Rome to escape their wrath. This tale does not, however, hold up under scrutiny. El Greco was, initially at least, an admirer of Michelangelo. A number of his early pictures clearly reveal a debt to the great Florentine, and in one of several versions of the *Purification of the Temple* he even included Michelangelo's face, along with portraits of Titian and Clovio, his first Roman benefactor.

We may never know the real reason why El Greco left Italy for Spain, but we can make some educated guesses. Although he was considered a painter of great promise by Clovio and Orsini, he failed to win any major commissions either in Rome or Venice. This must have been a factor in his decision to leave Italy and seek his fortune elsewhere. But why Spain? Among his friends in Rome were some Spanish clerics. They would have told him of the opportunities awaiting a painter in their homeland. Spain was the richest and most powerful realm on earth and its king, Philip II, was an indefatigable collector of art—particularly of Titians. El Greco probably felt that because of his association with Titian he stood a good chance of attracting the King's patronage.

El Greco arrived in Spain in 1577 and soon settled in Toledo. The city he would commemorate so often in his art was the ecclesiastical capital of Spain, and a cosmopolitan center as well. He quickly found friends and benefactors in the city's intellectual community. The artist was well qualified to move in such company; his library contained volumes in Greek, Latin, Italian and Spanish that ranged in subject from literature, philosophy and history to science, medicine and architecture.

In Toledo the field was wide open to him. There was no other painter of comparable talent around; nor was there another painter of his potential in all of Spain. Moreover, he had arrived at the right time. Under Philip II Spain stood convinced of its mission as defender of the faith. The Counter Reformation spirit had already produced an outpouring of ascetic and mystical literature. But the strivings of the Spanish soul had yet to be given expression in paint. Here, then, was El Greco's opportunity.

Within a year of his arrival he was busily at work. He had a commission for eight paintings to hang over the high altar and two side altars of the splendid new Church of Santo Domingo el Antiguo. In addition he had agreed to execute a large canvas for the sacristy of the Cathedral of Toledo. It took him no more than a couple of years to complete all nine works. The eight altarpieces for Santo Domingo el Antiguo demonstrate beyond question that El Greco's imagination took flame in Toledo. The four largest—*The Assumption of the Virgin, The Trinity, Adoration of the Shepherds* and *The Resurrection*—show him working with a certainty and an energy and a richness of color that clearly presage the development of a unique mode of expression.

It was with the *Espolio (page 93)*, his painting for the sacristy of the cathedral, however, that El Greco came into his own. He approached his theme, the disrobing of Christ, with a boldness that makes the *Espolio* one of the most original of all his works. He crowded the painting with figures that stand one in front of another and rise in a wall of bodies almost to the top of the canvas—and yet Jesus at the center remains powerfully and movingly the dramatic focus of the composition. A massive, cherry-red robe gives His large body monumentality. Gazing heavenward with liquid eyes, He seems oblivious of the mob around Him and even of His approaching martyrdom.

Magnificent though it is, the *Espolio* was almost immediately attacked by cathedral officials, whose motive may well have been to bring down the price. They complained that El Greco had shown disrespect by placing Christ on a level lower than that of the figures behind Him. They also criticized him for including the three Marys. The churchmen noted that scripture makes no mention of their presence at the disrobing (El Greco had apparently used as his source St. Bonaventure's *Meditations on the Passion,* which made them participants in the main action).

He agreed to "correct" the painting—but when he delivered the *Espolio,* he presented it exactly as he had conceived it, with none of the requested changes. At court hearings that followed to settle the payment, El Greco's independence of spirit was further revealed; in answer to what he obviously considered a superfluous question, he bluntly stated that he was "not obliged to give account" of his reasons for coming to Toledo. The fee that El Greco's representatives had set for the painting was 900 ducats; the appraisers for the cathedral valued it at only 227 ducats.

Chiefly known as a painter, El Greco created a number of sculptures, including this unusual nude *Risen Christ.* Carved in wood and painted, the small statue (it is just under 18 inches tall) shows none of the extreme elongation of the human body that is characteristic of El Greco's painted figures, but is more normally proportioned. The sculpture was completed in 1598, and within a few years El Greco repeated Christ's pose in his large painting *The Resurrection (page 96).* The statue was originally intended to stand upon the tabernacle of the high altar that El Greco designed for the Hospital of St. John the Baptist at Toledo.

HOSPITAL OF SAINT JOHN THE BAPTIST EXTRA MUROS, TOLEDO

The price finally agreed upon was 317 ducats, and this was doled out to the artist in small installments over a two-year period.

During these early years in Spain, El Greco suffered a much greater disappointment, one that dashed any hope he might have had of obtaining the regular patronage of Philip II. At first, everything went well. He executed a highly imaginative painting for the King, an allegorical depiction of the Holy League, the alliance of Spain, Venice and the Papacy against the infidel Turks. Philip liked it well enough to order another work, *The Martyrdom of St. Maurice*. Into this enormous canvas, measuring some 14 by 9 feet, El Greco poured his genius, obviously with the hope of solidifying Philip's favor. Employing a bold color scheme in which an ultramarine blue and a pale yellow dominate, he gave a quality of unearthliness to the scene of the martyrdom, and presented a personal vision of heaven. But the King apparently found the work too innovative. He paid El Greco for it, but hung another painting on the same theme in its designated place in the Escorial.

This incident must have convinced El Greco that his future lay not at the court but in Toledo. He had already put down roots there. Soon after settling in the city, he had met one Doña Jerónima de las Cuevas, who became his common-law wife. She gave birth in 1578 to a son, Jorge Manuel, who grew up to become a painter in his own right as well as his father's assistant and business partner. El Greco had begun to prosper in Toledo, but more important, he was increasingly inspired by his adopted city. A religious atmosphere as thick as incense hung over the town. Toledo had ceased to be the capital of Castile in 1560 and many people with purely secular interests had moved away, but it continued to be the seat of the Church in Spain. God ruled here. Less and less did El Greco look outward; in time he began to see another reality, a spiritual reality within himself. Painting became an act of faith, a way of communicating with God. As he gave shape to these feelings, he began to modify his style.

The change can be traced through El Greco's early work in Toledo. A painting of St. Sebastian, done sometime between 1577 and 1578, shows a conspicuous distortion of the human body; in it arms, legs and torso are attenuated. A *Crucifixion* executed two or three years later continues this trend. Christ's body is long and thin, like a dagger; nailed to the Cross, it nevertheless seems to twist and turn—almost as though it were about to fly away. The deep blue sky behind the Cross explodes in a tumult of gray clouds, driven every which way by a wind that blows from no one direction. In the elongation of the body and in the disregard of natural phenomena *The Crucifixion* is clearly not a picture of this world. El Greco had invented both a spiritual realm and a physical type with which to people it. He was but a step from one of his greatest and best-known paintings, the *Burial of Count Orgaz (pages 94 and 95)*.

In this painting El Greco depicted the miraculous moment when St. Augustine and St. Stephen appeared and lowered the count, a benefactor of the Church, into his tomb. He divided the composition in two, letting the bottom half represent the funeral, and the upper half the reception awaiting the soul of the nobleman in heaven. But even the scene on earth has its otherworldly aspects: there is little depth to it, and no ground line; nor is there any suggestion of a church interior beyond the flaming tapers held by various figures. The mourners are tightly packed together, but they seem unaware of one another as they meditate on life and death and the life everlasting. Their pale, ascetic faces mark the zone between heaven and earth, and are magnificently set off by white collars, the lace of which fairly sputters with quick strokes of El Greco's brush.

In its double view of heaven and earth, the *Burial of Count Orgaz* expresses two moods. The scene on earth, the burial, is subdued and somber. The scene in heaven is ecstatic; here El Greco used all his expressive powers to make the intangible tangible, the incomprehensible comprehensible. Colors—rose, blue, yellow—burn with bright intensity, and churning clouds, as thin as rose petals, bear aloft the host of angels and saints who stretch toward God. The figure of St. John the Baptist, to the right of the Virgin, is the most remarkable of all—a zigzag of attenuated limbs, lighted from on high by the reflected brilliance of Christ.

After this masterpiece, El Greco would never again be the same painter. His religious art became increasingly inspired. His brushstrokes licked like flames across his canvas. The proportions of his paintings changed; altarpieces grew narrower and taller. The figures in them strained upward toward heaven; colors took on acid pungency. Even El Greco's landscapes exuded a mystical quality. In his *View of Toledo (page 84)*, he edged the houses in silvery light and filled the sky and the land with movement. An event of great spiritual moment seems about to take place. Again and again he was to paint Toledo, even placing it at the feet of Christ in several versions of the Crucifixion. It is as if the city that had provided him his inspiration were also, somehow, the City of God.

How did El Greco's contemporaries react to his expressionistic style? Many admired it and understood it. In our own time the odd suggestion was made that El Greco distorted his figures because of imperfect vision —astigmatism. This theory fails to take into account the fact that he was not the only artist of the 16th Century to distort the human body. Members of the Mannerist school did so all the time; not surprisingly El Greco has often been called the last of the Mannerists. But he was much more. His distinction lay in taking what was essentially an artistic device and using it to make a wholly personal statement about his faith.

Throughout his career El Greco seems to have been a man of single-minded determination. Wherever he encountered personal injustice, he fought, and even his last years were marred by controversy. In 1603 he agreed to provide an altarpiece and several paintings for the church of the Hospital of Charity at Illescas, a town between Toledo and Madrid. These were to be ready within a little more than a year. Because of the magnitude of the commission, this proved impossible, and not until 1605 were the altarpiece and pictures finally in place. Shortly thereafter the trustees of the hospital issued a bill of complaint against the artist for his failure to meet their deadline, and a two-year wrangle over payment ensued when El Greco refused to accept the hospital's offer of a fee lower than that agreed upon.

All through the dispute, El Greco's output seems to have suffered.

But when the matter was settled—not, incidentally, to his advantage —he turned back to his easel. Among his new works was the *Adoration of the Shepherds (page 97)*, which he executed as his own memorial to be hung over his tomb in the Church of Santo Domingo el Antiguo. Spirit moves through the painting. The shepherds seem composed of vapor rather than substance. The light that illuminates them, a white phosphorescence, streams from the Christ Child, driving back darkness and making colors vibrate. The shoulder of the kneeling shepherd is a blaze of orange; the rest of his jacket, seen in shadow, is jet black. In a great outpouring of El Greco's emotion, paint travels restlessly over the surface of the canvas. There are no lines here; there seldom are in El Greco's paintings—only the routes traveled by his brushes. The elongation of the human body, so much his trademark, reaches a climax in the *Adoration,* where the towering figures clustered around the Christ Child express the glory of a reborn world.

El Greco died in April 1614. To those who knew him, his reputation seemed secured. But his star soon dimmed. This was due not only to his approach to art, which was far too personal for other artists to assimilate, but to a change in taste. Even before El Greco's death, Caravaggio's influence had been felt in Spain; realism was beginning to fascinate the new painters. Velázquez, still training at Pacheco's studio, had already clearly shown in his studies the direction his work was to take. Realism exactly suited his purposes, and would serve him well at the Madrid court. But there were others who hoped for the patronage of the churches and religious houses, and had to decide how they could adopt a realistic manner —and still make statements about faith as convincing as El Greco's. Among these painters were Ribera, Zurbarán and Murillo.

All three were born within a few years of Velázquez: Jusepe de Ribera in 1588, Francisco de Zurbarán in 1598 and Bartolomé Estéban Murillo in 1617. What they had in common was a fervent faith that remained unshaken as disillusionment began to shroud Spain's dreams. Ribera, the oldest, was the first to fall under the spell of realism. Almost all of his career was spent in Spanish-ruled Naples, where he was known as Il Spagnoletto, The Little Spaniard. During the first years of his stay in Italy, Ribera had worked as an etcher and painter in Rome, and there he had been exposed to the paintings of Caravaggio. The impact they had had on him was tremendous. Like Caravaggio, he illuminated his figures starkly and posed them in dark settings, as in his *St. Andrew (page 103)*. But as time wore on, he began to soften his lighting, to make less use of strong shadows and to brighten his backgrounds. One of his mightiest paintings in this manner is the *Martyrdom of St. Bartholomew (page 102),* in which the muscular saint and his torturers seem hewn from pale marble. Ribera never idealized the people he portrayed; many of his models were ordinary Neapolitans. With an etcher's concern for detail, he pored over his canvases. Skin took on the look of life; he made wrinkles by trailing single hairs of his brush in the wet paint. Yet for all the realism of his work, the religious content shines through; he seems to have found an inner life in his models, and let it show in their faces.

Ribera sought to make an essential statement about faith by casting plain people in the roles of saints and martyrs. Zurbarán attempted much the same thing, but his models were more special types—monks, for the most part. His paintings have a spareness; this reflects not only the ascetic tastes of his patrons, the monastic orders, but also, apparently, his upbringing and philosophical outlook. He was raised in Estremadura, a stark western province. At 15 he went to Seville for training, and then returned to Estremadura and settled in the town of Llerena. He stayed there 11 years before being invited by the Seville town council in 1629 to work in that city. He seems to have been very much affected by the Quietist movement. Among the tenets of the Quietists were "inner withdrawal," passivity, and "faith and silence in the presence of God."

Certainly quietude is one of the outstanding characteristics of Zurbarán's works. They have a clean, orderly quality; the needless has been eliminated. Colors are pure; whites glow. The Carthusians, the Capuchins and the Mercedarians whom he painted all wore white habits, and Zurbarán became a master at conveying the snowy brilliance of their robes. Looking at the slumped figure of St. Serapion *(page 98)*, a Mercedarian martyred in Africa, the viewer is likely to be struck not by the horror of the scene, but by the peacefulness of it—the utter stillness.

Whatever inner calm Zurbarán may have achieved was shattered when his second wife died in 1639. His output suffered, and his tone became more solemn. By the mid-1640s his popularity had begun to decline as the younger painter, Murillo, came to the fore. Increasingly, the older man was forced to depend upon the art market in the Spanish colonies for a living, and he was actually reduced at one point to selling colors and brushes from his studio. Attempting to recoup his losses, in 1658 he went to Madrid, where he died in 1664. With him died what little reputation he had left; like El Greco, he was not to be widely admired again until the 20th Century.

Murillo, who supplanted Zurbarán in Seville, exploded on the scene with 11 paintings done in 1645 and 1646 for the Franciscan monastery in Seville. Soon he was being paid 10 times what Zurbarán had received at his peak. Murillo's success stemmed not only from the freshness of his art, but from its warmth. He was, in the best sense of the phrase, the people's painter. He made the Virgin, Christ, Joseph and the saints not just holy but approachable. Like Ribera, he found his models among ordinary men, women and children. But in his selection he was guided by a sense of beauty; his Virgins are invariably lovely girls.

After starting out under the influence of both Zurbarán and Ribera, Murillo perfected his own manner. His work became characterized by harmony and gracefulness. The mood he most often conveyed was one of sweetness, and at times he was unabashedly sentimental. His reputation continued long after his death in 1682, and he was even thought of as the world's greatest painter. The 20th Century has chosen to see him differently. There are people today who call him saccharine and dismiss him—but this is to overlook the joy contained in his art, the reflection of a serene state of mind as rare in his day as it is in ours. It was a state of mind increasingly denied his fellow Sevillian, Diego Velázquez, at work in the court close to power—and chaos.

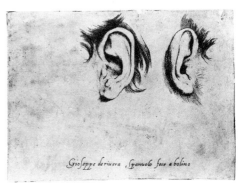

Velázquez' great contemporary Jusepe de Ribera was a masterful draftsman. His skill is evident in the etching below, a meticulously detailed study of the head of a sick old man. His passion for realistic rendering also led Ribera to produce dozens of drawings of parts of the body, like those above, which were etched in 1622 and intended for the use of student artists.

Painters of an Intense Faith

In the highly charged religious atmosphere of Spain, Velázquez was the only major artist who dealt primarily with secular subjects. Sacred themes dominated the work of the eminent painters, including Velázquez' best-known contemporaries, Zurbarán, Murillo and Ribera. Their styles varied: Zurbarán's was severe, Murillo's charming and Ribera's starkly realistic. But all three followed their predecessors in concentrating on such subjects as the Annunciation, the Adoration and the Resurrection, and in portraying saints and martyrs. They gave these themes a passion not to be found in other European art. That Spaniards excelled in fervor is hardly surprising: Spain, stronghold of the Inquisition and spearhead of the Counter Reformation, was pervaded by a religious zeal that bordered on ecstasy. Zurbarán, Murillo and Ribera shared and made manifest this spirit.

A generation earlier Spain had been home to a great master of religious subjects, one of the towering figures in Western art. He was Domenikos Theotokopoulos, known as El Greco—The Greek. Born in Crete, trained in Italy, El Greco was in his mid-thirties when he settled permanently in the intensely pious city of Toledo. Spain suited him; the mysticism, melancholy and reality of her faith deeply stirred his genius. Under the influence of the religious dedication of his adopted homeland, El Greco, more than any artist in history, made visible on canvas the spiritual content of Christianity.

El Greco combined elements of three worlds—Crete, Italy and Spain—when he painted the *Espolio (Disrobing of Christ)* *(right)*. The glowing colors are reminiscent of the jewel-encrusted Byzantine icons of Crete, his birthplace. The foreshortened youth, a mass of muscles in the right foreground, suggests the influence of Michelangelo. The Roman soldier is clad as a captain in the army of Spain, the country of El Greco's artistic maturity.

El Greco: *Espolio (Disrobing of Christ)*, 1577-1579

El Greco: *Burial of Count Orgaz,* 1586-1588

In this towering 15-by-11-foot canvas, El Greco depicts the entombment of a noble benefactor of a Toledo church, the Count of Orgaz. According to local legend, St. Stephen and St. Augustine descended from heaven to place the count's body in its crypt. Here the brilliantly robed saints perform their miracle; simultaneously, the count's soul—represented by the baby held in the arms of an angel—ascends to heaven. El Greco relied on his imagination to portray the population of paradise, but at the line of demarcation between heaven and earth he painted a group of realistic portraits of living people, members of Toledo's aristocracy *(detail, right).* Among them he may have placed himself. He is possibly the man gazing out of the picture in left center, his face directly above the gesturing hand. At lower left, also peering outward, is El Greco's eight-year-old son, Jorge Manuel.

94

The lifelike portraits in the *Burial of Count Orgaz* marked the apex of realism in El Greco's religious works. Henceforth the visionary absorbed him, and he expressed it vividly in the two masterpieces on these pages. The elongated, straining figures in *The Resurrection (right)* have no duplicates in human reality; nor have human bodies ever glimmered with such blues, reds and yellows. Even when El Greco elected to paint Christ's adoration by shepherds *(far right)*—an event that particularly lends itself to realistic portrayal—the painter avoided simple factual representation. The worshipful figures are recognizably human but as they realize that they have come upon the Christ Child, they writhe and assume fantastic postures. In distorting them, El Greco magnificently conveys his own sense of awe in the presence of the divine.

El Greco: *The Resurrection*, c. 1600-1605

El Greco: *Adoration of the Shepherds,* 1612-1614

97

Francisco de Zurbarán: *St. Serapion*, 1628

Among Velázquez' contemporaries, the most deeply religious artist was Francisco de Zurbarán, who once spent months sharing the ascetic life of one of the monastic orders that provided the bulk of his commissions. For the Mercedarians he executed this moving study of St. Serapion, a 13th Century martyr. The saint wears the Order's white habit, a costume that Zurbarán was adept at portraying; he was a superb technician who could depict folds of white as "crisp as frozen snow, soft as cotton, heavy as cream." The depth of feeling that emanates from the tragic *St. Serapion* also appears in the painting of the young Virgin at right. But she is no somber figure. The interplay of the black, white and red of her dress demonstrates that Zurbarán was colorist in addition to stylist; more important, the *Virgin* shows that he could convey tenderness as well as martyrdom. Draperies frame a domestic scene. But the ethereal light and the wistful expression on her seemingly translucent face elevate this picture from simple portraiture to an expression of devotion, a virtual prayer in paint.

Francisco de Zurbarán: *The Young Virgin*, c. 1632

Bartolomé Estéban Murillo: *The Holy Family of the Little Bird*, 1645-1650

The Christ Child plays with a puppy; St. Joseph joins in the frolic; the Virgin, a basket of household linen at her feet, stops winding a ball of yarn to watch her son. The sentimentality of this depiction of the Holy Family typifies the style of Bartolomé Estéban Murillo. The same overlay of sweetness is seen in his picture of the two urchins at right. Murillo's homespun approach to his themes, both religious and secular, made him famous in his lifetime, but his success was not based solely on the appeal of sentimentality. Murillo had a particularly gentle and deft touch with the faces of children, whether the subjects were heavenly or earthly. And, as the shifting

Bartolomé Estéban Murillo: *The Grape and Melon Eaters*, c. 1650-1660

shades of gold, red and blue in these pictures show, he was a master colorist. Perhaps of deeper significance is Murillo's expression of the typical Spanish concern with the tragedy that may lie behind appearances. His urchins seem carefree, but they are really impoverished boys forced to scratch for a living in the streets. Similarly, *The*

Holy Family is not simply a rendering of the pleasures of domesticity. The goldfinch in the boy's raised hand foretells agony: the goldfinch, a bird that eats only thorny plants, traditionally represents the Crown of Thorns that, in turn, symbolizes the Passion. The painting, therefore, is a reminder of the future awaiting the young Jesus.

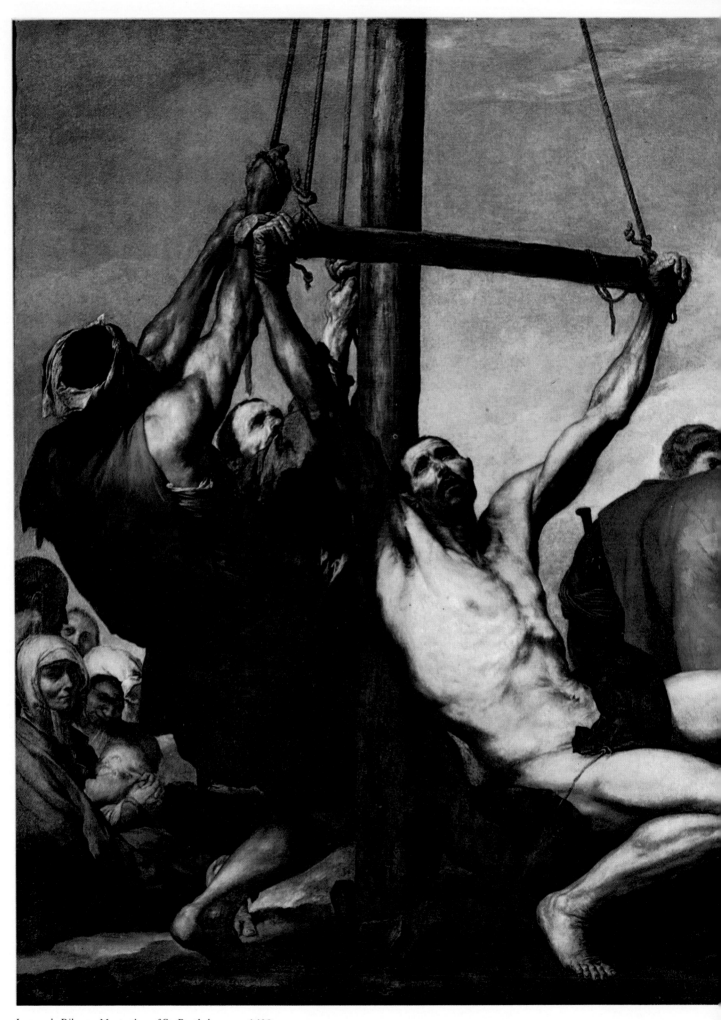

Jusepe de Ribera: *Martyrdom of St. Bartholomew*, c. 1630

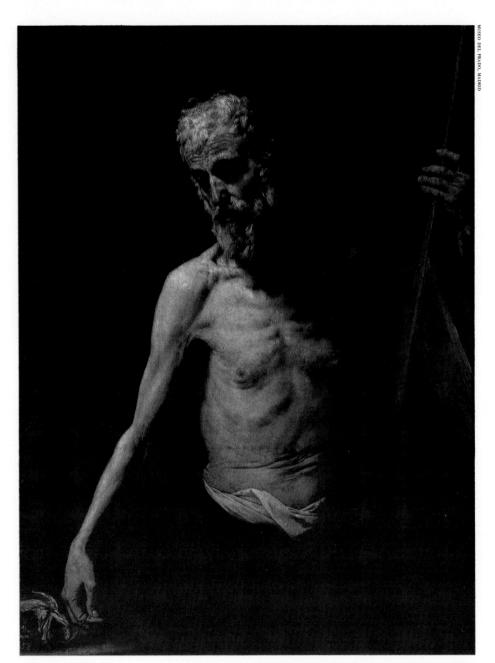

Jusepe de Ribera: *St. Andrew*, c. 1635

Unlike Murillo, Jusepe de Ribera never sentimentalized his sitters—or his themes. Born in Valencia, he spent most of his life in Spanish-ruled Naples, claiming that "Spain was a pious mother to strangers but a cruel stepmother to her own children." In Naples, he painted *St. Bartholomew (left)*, the martyr who had been the bridegroom at the wedding in Cana, where Jesus transformed water into wine. The saint is pictured as his tormentors prepared to flay him. Yet, despite his imminent martyrdom, he remains human. Under the anguish on his face is visible the strong character of the local fisherman or dockworker who posed for the painting. When Ribera executed his *St. Andrew (above)*, the model's weathered face and withered torso apparently intrigued the painter as much as the sanctity of the apostle he was portraying. St. Andrew too is real, as real as was the mystery of faith to the painters of Spain.

103

V

The King
Takes Command

One of the mysteries surrounding Velázquez is his relatively meager output. In a career that spanned some 43 years he produced no more than 162 known paintings; of these, 111 survive. His contemporaries Zurbarán and Murillo, working under seemingly less ideal conditions, produced several hundred canvases each. Curiously, Velázquez' output began to decline just as he hit his stride—in 1635, when he was 36 and had finished his paintings for the Hall of Realms. In the decade that followed he turned out only a dozen-and-a-half known works, mostly portraits. Several of them, including a new portrait of Philip IV *(left),* rank among his best. But the fact remains that during what are often the most productive years of a man's life Velázquez painted comparatively little. What held him back?

An obvious answer is that he was busy with other matters. He was, after all, not only court painter but a courtier as well, with certain functions to fulfill; in 1636, for example, he became a Gentleman of the Wardrobe, an honorary position but one that may have required him to trail after the King on the royal peregrinations from one place to another. But perhaps there was something else that kept Velázquez from his easel. These were particularly agonizing years for Spain, years of war abroad and at home, of growing dissension, poverty and financial crisis. There were moments when things looked bright, but there were long stretches when they looked very bleak, and when the King and his mainstay, Olivares, seemed simply to flail at problems rather than deal effectively with them. The shortcomings of both men became increasingly apparent; Olivares, indeed, was finally to fall from power. Velázquez, who could observe the inadequacies of his king and the Minister at close hand, may have grown depressed and unmotivated.

This fateful decade, ironically, opened on a high note for Spain. The military power of the Protestant foe in Europe had appeared to be broken in 1634 at the Battle of Nördlingen, in Germany, and to all intents and purposes the Thirty Years' War should have been over. The hero of Nördlingen was Philip's brother Fernando. He was on his way north from Italy with his troops to assume the governorship of Flanders when he received a plea from his Habsburg cousin and Spain's ally, the Holy Roman Emperor Ferdinand II, for assistance against a large Protestant force under Swedish-German command. Fernando arrived at Nördlingen just in time to help turn what could easily have become a rout for the imperial troops into a victory.

But peace, which now became a genuine prospect, was something Spain's longtime rival, France, could not permit. Cardinal Richelieu, the astute French Minister, was well aware of the danger to his country of a resurgent Spain freed of her involvement in the Thirty Years' War. If she were no longer drained by costly military expenditures, she might eventually realize her dreams of hegemony over Europe—and France would be caught in the middle between two Habsburg dominions, Spain and Austria. Richelieu had long worked behind the scenes to frustrate Spanish ambitions. After Nördlingen, however, he was left with no choice but to come out in the open, and in May 1635 France declared war on Philip and Ferdinand II. Spain found herself threatened in two key areas. One was the border shared by the recalcitrant province of Catalonia with France, across which an attack might come at any time. The other was Flanders, where Fernando—so recently hailed as the hero of Nördlingen—was forced to adopt a defensive position.

It was soon tested and found vulnerable. In July 1635 news reached Madrid that Fernando had suffered a severe defeat at the hands of the French in Flanders, and that, moreover, he had been in great danger personally. The King was deeply upset. When he also learned that Fernando had written home for aid, and that Olivares had deliberately withheld the letter because no aid could be sent, he became furious and gave his Minister a tongue-lashing. This was a rare display of independence for the King, and an omen that Olivares might well have noted. But Philip's anger proved short-lived, and Olivares—for a time, at least—remained as powerful as ever.

With characteristic energy Olivares set about mustering the additional men and money required by the new downturn in Spain's military fortunes. The task, as he knew perhaps better than anyone, was a formidable one. Spaniards had been fighting for one cause or another since 1621 and were exhausted; starvation was becoming common not only in the crop-poor countryside but in Madrid. Private means were dwindling. Already Olivares had gone directly to the people for a *donativo*. The rich had been obliged to dig deep into their pockets, and even the poor had been expected to give. Later 2,000 of Madrid's 3,300 beggars were actually removed from their "public mendicancy" status, presumably so that they could be asked to contribute as well.

Impoverishment was by no means restricted to the lower classes; when one aristocrat's coaches and horses were seized because he had failed to pay a fine for some offense, it was discovered that they did not belong to him; nor, for that matter, did the fine furnishings and tapestries in his home. All had been rented. The Crown's own finances were in a precarious state. Many courtiers went unpaid, Velázquez among them. When, in 1636, he applied for two years' back wages, clothing allowance and payments due on his pictures, he got scant satisfaction; it took four years more before the King finally decreed a 500-ducat annual fee for him, covering all future works as well as those done in the past.

Seemingly there were no resources, public or private, left for Olivares to tap in raising funds for the war against the French. Still, he not only imposed new taxes but seized the interest from government bonds held by individuals. He also compelled all local government offices to buy stationery from the Crown at inflated prices. Anyone caught counterfeiting this specially marked paper was to be put to death. As a last resort, Olivares appropriated from the rightful owners 487,000 ducats' worth of treasure brought from the colonies by the Silver Fleet (two years later he would confiscate one million ducats' worth).

The same drastic approach marked Olivares' recruiting of manpower. The problems on this score were no less difficult. Observing the first results, the English Ambassador reported that the hapless Spaniards pressed into the infantry were so loath to go that they had to be "carried like galley slaves." Even the horses, he added, were so weak that they were unlikely to make it to the battlefield. Olivares blandly ignored these obstacles and pursued his goal of a 40,000-man army to be stationed in Catalonia for deployment against the foe as the need arose. He also devised a long-term strategy that called for, among other things, a three-pronged drive on France from Catalonia, Flanders and Austria.

It was a grandiose plan, conceived by a grandiose man, but in a memorandum to the King outlining the strategy, Olivares revealed the desperation behind the façade. Appending his own remarkably candid appraisal of the situation, he wrote: "To my mind this will lose everything irremediably or be the salvation of the ship. Here go religion, king, kingdom, nation, everything, and, if our strength is insufficient, let us die in the attempt. Better to die . . . than to fall under the dominion of others, and most of all heretics, as I consider the French to be. Either all is lost, or else Castile will be the head of the world, as it is already head of Your Majesty's Monarchy."

The sheer bravado of this declaration may have helped stir the King from his lethargy. Philip professed himself as ready as his Minister to risk everything. Perhaps inspired by Fernando's example, he announced his determination to lead his troops personally into battle. Ostensibly Olivares approved of the decision; actually, rumor held, he was not eager for the King to leave Madrid—and escape his influence. In any event, the euphoria of both King and Minister soon vanished. In the summer of 1636 Fernando, having rallied from his defeat in Flanders, drove deep into France; but, lacking reinforcements, he stopped short of Paris, giving the French the breathing spell they needed. Fernando was forced to fall back to his Flemish base and thus was dashed any hope of an early end to the war.

Philip continued to proclaim his thirst for combat, but he remained in Madrid amid the agreeable comforts of the Buen Retiro. Often he was depressed and showed it; at such times his courtiers would scurry to lift his sagging spirits, devising all manner of distractions to keep his mind off the war. As a result life at court was, if anything, gayer and more lavish than before. Many of those who shared in it must have known that

Spain stood at a critical juncture in her fortunes, but the face they presented to the world was carefree.

Part of the pretense consisted of costly entertainments saluting lofty foreign visitors; what better means of persuading the rest of Europe that all was well in Madrid? One celebration—outdoing, people proudly said, even the spectacles of ancient Rome—was held to honor, in absentia, the newly elected Holy Roman Emperor Ferdinand III, Philip's cousin and brother-in-law. The cost for candles on one evening alone amounted to more than 6,000 ducats, and the expense of a single feast came to a staggering 500,000 ducats. "The charge hath certainly been very great," an English eyewitness observed, "but hath cost the King nothing; for it hath long [been the practice] for this town to defray all extraordinaries either for his honor and/or his pleasure." Some Spaniards themselves easily rationalized the expenditure. One of them wrote: "This great event, which had no other end than pastime and pleasure . . . was to show our friend Cardinal Richelieu that there is plenty more money left in the world to punish his king."

There were other pinpricks for the hated Cardinal in the form of elaborate welcomes for his known enemies. One visitor was the Bourbon Princess of Carignano, one of his most blue-blooded critics. Hard on her heels, in December 1637, came another lady, the Duchess of Chevreuse, who had escaped from Richelieu's agents, and whose presence in Madrid, according to one Spanish official, was even more of a triumph "than if we had won and seized three important French strongholds." The Madrileños were especially taken with the Duchess. "She is very lovely, pink and white," one wrote, "and has at the same time a majestic and sweet appearance." She seems to have been a free spirit who wore daringly low-cut dresses. Velázquez painted her "in her French costume with her French graces." The portrait, which must have been all the more intriguing for the Duchess' décolletage, was later lost. It is a disappearance to be regretted, for Velázquez could paint women enchantingly, as is evidenced in *Lady with a Fan (page 149)*.

Soon after the departure of the lovely Duchess, still another distinguished foreigner arrived at court, the Duke of Modena and Reggio. The Duke, too, was painted by Velázquez. The portrait is a half-length, and shows a self-possessed young Italian nobleman, but its chief interest lies in some correspondence that survives about it. Velázquez undertook it not on the King's behalf—as a graceful favor to an honored guest—but at the Duke's own order, and for a fee; with courtiers' salaries so uncertain, he was apparently happy to earn a little extra money. But he had to agree to take it in installments. Evidently the ducal emissary at court who insisted on this arrangement feared that the painter would procrastinate. He was proved right; the portrait was not yet completed when the Duke departed for home. In a progress report the emissary declared that Velázquez had "the defect of other famous men, namely, never to finish and never to tell the truth." But then, having delivered himself of this barb, he ended on a note of high praise. Velázquez, he assured the Duke, "is expensive, but does good work . . . in his portraits I do not esteem him inferior to any others more renowned among the an-

A Flemish merchant traveling through Philip IV's Spain wrote that even in the smallest villages he found men avidly playing cards. These ubiquitous decks consisted of 40 cards in four suits: swords, coins, clubs and cups *(shown above, clockwise from upper left)*. The national rage was called *hombre,* a complicated game that is still played in Spain. Most cards were imported from France—an expense willingly borne by the poorest Spaniards, who evidently found in cards and games of chance a welcome diversion from the hardships of daily life.

cients or the moderns." The Duke was plainly of the same opinion. He is said to have been so pleased with the portrait when he finally received it that he supplemented the fee with the gift of a gold chain, which Velázquez thereafter wore on festive occasions.

In time more thoughtful Madrileños began to tire of the steady stream of visiting dignitaries. One of them ruefully complained, "each day new guests come who cost us more than the army." But this was a grievance that could be aired only in private. On the surface, at least, the gaiety at court went on apace, heedless of troubles abroad, indifferent to those closer to home. Early one morning a fire swept the Buen Retiro, forcing the King to scramble naked into the gardens. Two days passed before the blaze could be wholly extinguished, and many costly art objects—possibly including a few paintings by Velázquez—were destroyed. But both the theater and the Hall of Realms escaped damage, and within another two days King and courtiers were back to attend a new play and discuss the rebuilding of the palace. Again collectors were asked to give generously of their most prized possessions to refurnish the rooms, and the various administrative bodies of Castile were called upon to donate the 120,000 ducats required for repairs.

One of the most curious aspects of this court that played while the country starved and war drew ever nearer the gates was its perennial fascination with the dwarfs and fools who by tradition formed a part of the royal retinue. Perhaps they lent a touch of sanity in the prevailing insanity; they had a reputation for speaking the truth under the guise of madness. They often attended Philip at mealtimes and the theater, traveled with him on occasion, and appeared with him at audiences and festivals; during the Duke of Modena's visit in 1638, for example, two dwarfs dressed as Castilian kings sat on the steps of the throne while Philip and his guest watched a bullfight. No one saw any offense to the monarchy in this, or in the fact that the dwarfs and fools sometimes mimicked the King and other important personages. As members of Philip's household they enjoyed financial and clothing allowances. The dwarfs, in addition, had the right to keep their hats on in the presence of the King. Some lent themselves to court intrigues and thereby gained special favors.

Velázquez knew the dwarfs and fools well, and painted several of them, beginning with the little cross-eyed jester known as Calabazas, and ending with Mari-Bárbola, the cabbage-headed hydrocephalic in *Las Meninas*. His portraits of these unfortunates are among his most moving works, and they show a steady deepening of his humanity. When he portrayed Calabazas for the first time, around 1628 or 1629, he gave the jester a winsome air; when he painted him again in the late 1630s he saw him with compassion *(pages 128 and 129)*. In this predominantly black-and-white portrait, Calabazas—the nickname means "gourds," symbol of empty-headedness—sits hunched upon a low stool. Gaiety shines through his dull features; he seems anxious to please with what little he has to offer. He is utterly defenseless in his subservience—completely trapped by his need to amuse people. Velázquez painted his eyes in soft focus, veiling them in shadow, making the pupils smudges of black, thus heightening the poignancy of their appealing gaze.

Hunchbacks, and dwarfs like those Velázquez painted in Philip's court, enjoyed a special place in 17th Century European society; they usually found a living as entertainers. Jacques Callot, a leading French engraver, pictured these two—one making a toast, the other strumming a mandolin—in Florence. Callot's deft etchings show his subjects as grotesque figures working to get a laugh; he had little of Velázquez' empathy for them as human beings. Yet each artist, with his own eye for detail, reveals the character of an often brutish age.

Velázquez' sense of decency was, in fact, one of his greatest attributes, and it emerged as much when he was painting a dwarf as when portraying a king. He never failed to see a subject as a human being, nor did he ever draw a moral judgment. He valued people for what they were, and he painted them as they let themselves be seen. Perhaps the most touching of all his portraits is that of the hydrocephalic cretin, Francisco Lezcano (pages 132 and 133), the companion of Prince Baltasar Carlos. Velázquez showed him sitting on the ground, a deck of cards in his stubby hands, one foot with its thick-soled shoe thrusting directly at the viewer. Lezcano has thrown back his swollen head and smiles. Surely this is the most pathetic smile ever painted, reflecting all the agony of the human condition. Lezcano is a being overwhelmed by his own ugliness; his distorted body seems to wrestle with his soul and drag it to the ground. And yet there is bravery here—and a touch of defiance.

In painting Philip's dwarfs, Velázquez may have been giving vent to some of his own feelings about the court and his position in it. His portrait of Sebastian de Morra (pages 130 and 131) reflects suppressed rage—the dwarf's certainly, and perhaps also Velázquez' own. De Morra sits on the floor, his short legs stick straight out, and his thick hands are tightly bunched into fists. This awkward pose makes him look like a doll stuck up on a shelf—the plaything he in fact was. But one glimpse of de Morra's intense face and black, angry eyes is enough to convince the viewer that he detested his role, that he wanted to be regarded as a human being, not as a toy.

Apart from any emotional release they offered him, Velázquez' paintings of dwarfs and fools may also have provided him with the chance to try out new techniques that he could employ later in his other portraits. Thus his painting of the buffoon Don Juan of Austria, executed perhaps as early as 1632 or 1633, heralds in the thinness of its paint and the freedom of its brushwork the watercolor look of much of Velázquez' later work. His boldly executed portrait of another buffoon, Pablo de Valladolid (page 121), produced in the mid-1630s, shows other evidences of experimentation. Not only was Valladolid's theatrical pose a departure, but so was the undifferentiated space in which the jester stands. There is no floor line to suggest a measurable distance, nor is there a backdrop of any kind. More than two centuries later, the French artist Édouard Manet, a fervent admirer of Velázquez' work, pointed out the enormous difficulty "of placing a single figure on the canvas and concentrating all interest on this solitary figure, retaining, all the while, its lifelikeness and body."

The biggest project to absorb Velázquez during this period of forced gaiety grew out of the King's decision to rebuild and decorate his tower-shaped hunting lodge outside Madrid, the Torre de la Parada. That a project of such scope should have been undertaken at all at this luckless time for Spain says much about its monarch's essential weakness. Presumably Philip had spoken in all sincerity when he declared his intention to go off to the war; presumably, also, he realized his country's economic plight. And yet, although the palatial Buen Retiro had only recently been completed, he gave urgent priority to the remodeling of the royal lodge. Both the project and the place provided the distraction Philip so desperately sought. Hunting was his favorite sport; he could spend as many as 12 hours a day at it, never tiring, laughing at his exhausted beaters and gunbearers. No doubt it did him good to be reminded that he excelled at something. He was widely regarded as Spain's bravest hunter. He was indisputably active at the sport; in one year alone he is supposed to have bagged 150 boars, 400 wolves and 600 deer.

For the scene of such personal glory none but the best would do, and the plans for the Torre de la Parada were lavish. The paintings called for in the scheme of decoration required the services of a number of artists. One of them was the aging Peter Paul Rubens, still at the height of his European fame. He alone provided some 40 oil sketches for the hunting lodge, although many of the actual paintings based on them were executed by his assistants.

Velázquez may have been given the task of selecting the works of the painters and deciding how they were to be arranged at the lodge; such an assignment would have been appropriate to his dual role of courtier and court painter. In any event, he himself produced several paintings for the Torre de la Parada. Three were life-sized portraits of Philip, Fernando and Baltasar Carlos, all dressed for the hunt, with hounds at their feet. Two more were portrayals of a very different sort and subject, not elegant, but down-to-earth—two celebrated figures of ancient Greece, Menippus and Aesop *(pages 112 and 113)*. Velázquez painted both figures as though they had just stepped off the dusty streets of Madrid into his studio. Aesop, the storyteller, has a weary, resigned look; Menippus, the philosopher, wears a sardonic grin. Clearly each knows what life is all about; each projects an air of rugged competence.

Among other works Velázquez is believed to have produced for the Torre de la Parada is one called *Mars*. As in his earlier mythological paintings, *Bacchus* and *The Forge of Vulcan*, he again portrayed a god in a very real, very human light. Indeed, he may well have been poking fun at the god of war, whom the poet Quevedo called "a celestial Don Quixote." Mars is seated on what looks like a studio prop, naked to the waist; his most conspicuous item of clothing is his unstrapped helmet, which projects out over his forehead and casts a shadow over his eyes, nose and large walrus mustache. He has tossed aside his shield and armor, and partially supports himself with his staff. He seems tired, bored—too weary to fight. In another moment the god of war may drowse off and topple from his perch.

If there is a trace of cynicism in *Mars, Menippus* and *Aesop*, there is none whatever in Velázquez' portrait of his king as hunter. It is perhaps the most dashing and attractive of all of Velázquez' studies of the monarch *(page 123)*. As always in the King's case, the artist went to considerable pains with this portrait. He was not entirely satisfied with the first try, and made a number of changes. The areas he repainted can be easily picked out today, since the pigment underneath has worked up to the surface in a kind of double-exposure effect—as at the King's hip, where the ghost of a cap may be seen. But the spirited portrayal remains. Philip, clad in his favorite brown, a long gun in his right hand, his left

Among the paintings that Velázquez made for the King's hunting lodge, the Torre de la Parada, were these imposing, life-sized portraits of the ancient Greek writers Menippus *(right)* and Aesop *(opposite page)*. Aesop's *Fables* were widely known and loved in Spain; they are mentioned by Sancho Panza in Cervantes' *Don Quixote*. The painter shows Aesop standing over a tanner's bucket and hides, an allusion to one of his fables about a rich man who learned equanimity in the face of personal discomfort—in his case the stench from a tannery next door. Menippus the cynic, considered a Classical forerunner of Cervantes, is shown with some of the books he satirized strewn about his feet.

hand on his hip, stands gracefully against a gray-green landscape. He is the very picture of insouciance, a ruler seemingly without a single trouble in all the world.

Precisely what year this portrait was painted is not known, but it was sometime during the course of the Torre de la Parada project that a new and unprecedented type of trouble did, indeed, beset Philip. It involved a young woman, and thanks to the absolutist nature of the monarchy it was hushed up; yet even in that dissolute milieu it was an extraordinary scandal and no one can judge the extent of the damage it did to the morale of the court, and to Velázquez' faith in his sovereign's fiber.

According to one version of the much-whispered story, word came to Philip through a henchman of Olivares', Don Jerónimo de Villanueva, that there was a lovely new nun at the Convent of San Placido in Madrid. The King's zest for the chase not being limited to the outdoors, he went to see the nun and became so smitten that nothing would do but that he have her. Arrangements for a meeting were made forthwith. Conveniently, Villanueva's house adjoined the convent. A passage was cut through into the convent cellar. There in a small, dark room the King's tryst was to take place. But the nun told her mother superior about the plan, and on the appointed day Philip entered the room to find the nun stretched out on a cushioned dais like a funeral bier, with her eyes closed and a crucifix and candles heightening the eerie effect. After one glimpse the King fled. The story of his visit leaked out, however, and came to the ears of the Inquisition. Philip, conscience-stricken, was apparently ready to take whatever humiliation might be meted out. But Olivares, who had also been involved, could not allow this without jeopardizing his own position. Olivares forced the Inquisitor-General of the Holy Office into retirement and arranged for the interception of accusatory papers that were already en route to the Pope. These were brought back to Spain and burned in the King's private apartments, and the scandal, if not its aftertaste, subsided.

Among those who appear not to have been overly upset by the King's latest and most shocking peccadillo was, interestingly enough, the Queen. By now she was used to his frailties. Strange as it may seem, she was devoted to her husband and he to her. They had common interests, and they shared a common tragedy. With conjugal regularity, the Queen had gone on bearing a new baby almost every other year. But of five girls and two boys, only Baltasar Carlos had lived beyond infancy. The losses took their toll, and in 1637 Isabel lapsed into a deep depression. In 1638, however, she gave birth to another child, María Teresa—and this little girl lived. Velázquez painted her at least three times. Ironically, after the war with France ended, she was to become the bride of its illustrious young monarch, Louis XIV.

But in 1638 no one could have predicted this outcome. That summer Richelieu made his first big attack on Spanish soil, capturing Irún and the harbor of Pasages and laying siege to the fortress of Fuenterrabía in northern Spain (map, page 10). A relief force assembled by Olivares broke the siege. The victory was hailed in Madrid as Olivares' own, although he had not been near the battlefield. Philip showered him with honors and made him a general. Velázquez' portrait of Olivares on horseback, with an impressionistically rendered battle scene in the background (page 77), shows him in the role of commander in chief of the armies.

Perhaps a more persuasive portrait of a military personality, painted by Velázquez at about the same time, was that of the Captain General of the Spanish Navy, Admiral Adrián Pulido Pareja. The portrait is now lost, but it must have been a remarkable essay in realism. Palomino, Velázquez' early biographer, reported that after finishing the work, the artist stood it in a dark corner of his studio. One day the King came to the studio "as was his custom" to watch the artist paint. Spotting the portrait in the shadows, Philip took it for Pareja himself. "What!" he said. "Are you still here? Have I not already sent you off?" Then, realizing his error, Philip turned to Velázquez, "who was modestly pretending not to take notice," and said, "I assure you that I deceived myself."

The victory at Fuenterrabía, though encouraging, was only temporary, and the war dragged on. Olivares found himself faced not only by a lack of competent officers, but an increasing shortage of money and manpower. When the French again invaded Catalonia in 1639, capturing Salces, a fortress on the frontier, Olivares was hard put to assemble a retaliatory force. He had never given up hope of uniting the provinces of Spain in his Union of Arms, and he used the invasion as the cudgel with which to involve the Catalans directly in the affairs of the monarchy. He ordered his viceroy in Catalonia to mobilize the province for war. Men were drafted, supplies were appropriated, and an army was sent to Salces. For six months, under the most trying conditions, Catalans and non-Catalans besieged the fortress. Desertions ran high. Enraged by what he took to be a sign of Catalan treachery, Olivares began disregarding the Catalans' constitutional rights, claiming that the defense of the country took priority. He also saddled the already hard-pressed Catalans with heavier taxes and forced them to billet his 9,000-man army over the winter. With his usual bluntness he urged his viceroy to "take great care that the troops are well lodged and have good beds, and if there are none to be had, you must not hesitate to take them from the highest people in the province; for it is better that they should lie on the ground than that the troops should suffer."

The Catalans had had all they could bear, and in May 1640 they rose in rebellion. A month later an angry mob killed Olivares' hand-picked viceroy. The Catalans then renounced Philip as their king and turned to his enemy, Louis XIII of France, as their protector.

Another major blow was dealt the Crown when, on December 1, 1640, Portugal declared itself an independent kingdom under the rule of the Duke of Braganza. It, too, had had all it could take of Olivares' demands. Philip was watching a bullfight when the report of the revolt arrived in Madrid. Olivares waited until the King had returned to the palace to break the news—and then in a most artful fashion. "I bring you great news for your Majesty," he announced.

"What is it?" asked Philip.

"In one moment, Sire, you have won a great dukedom and vast wealth."

"How so?"

"Sire, the Duke of Braganza has gone mad, and has proclaimed himself King of Portugal; so it will be necessary for you to confiscate all his possessions."

"Let a remedy be found for it," was the King's laconic reply.

But the time was coming when the King could no longer be deluded by his Minister. Many nobles had already withdrawn from the court in a boycott of Olivares. Some people were bold enough to try to reach Philip's ear—and some, in spite of Olivares' surveillance, managed to get through to him. Among these was the poet Quevedo. The story goes that he wrote a diatribe against Olivares' policies and slipped it under Philip's table napkin for him to read—and was thrown into prison for his pains. But Philip would have been an utter idiot if he had been unable to take stock of the situation himself. The realm was being squeezed dry of money. Inflation was rendering the copper coinage worthless. Crime proliferated; during one two-week period, 110 murders occurred in Madrid alone. "The agony and desperation of the people were intense," wrote an observer, "and utter despair consumed hearts and lives." From Catalonia and elsewhere came news of one defeat after another. Olivares himself was gloomy; as early as March 1640 he had written to Philip: "God

One of the most interesting political figures Velázquez painted was Don Francisco de Quevedo y Villegas, a poet and writer whose early support for Philip's First Minister Olivares turned to outspoken opposition and landed the poet in jail. The work above is a copy of Velázquez' lost original. The eyeglasses that make Quevedo appear so scholarly became such a trademark that the word "quevedos" is now Spanish for "spectacles." In spite of being shortsighted and lame, Quevedo was an active sportsman, kept several mistresses and did not hesitate to fight a duel when the occasion demanded.

wants us to make peace, for He is depriving us visibly and absolutely of all the means of war."

Spain's literary titan, Cervantes, compared the 17th Century to "a fool garnished with understanding who has a few lucid moments." So, too, Philip had his few moments beginning in 1642. Things had gone from bad to disastrous: his brother Fernando had died in Flanders, and reinforcements on the way to the Catalonian front for a last-ditch effort against the French had been overwhelmed and destroyed. Madrid was in a panic. The French now were in a position to drive into Aragon, and their king, Louis XIII, was already in the Rossellón, a region in northern Catalonia. Almost seven years had passed since Philip had first announced his intention to lead his army in person. Now he would have to take command. The royal honor demanded it.

Somehow men were mustered, and on April 26 the King set out with Olivares and a large entourage of courtiers for Catalonia, leaving the Queen in charge in Madrid as regent. The route Philip took to war, however, was meandering, with so much time spent visiting shrines and the houses of noblemen along the way that he did not reach Saragossa, the capital of Aragon, until July 27. By then French raiders had penetrated deep into Aragon from Catalonia, and there was real concern for the King's safety. He was kept a virtual prisoner in his quarters by Olivares, and the only combat he witnessed at this time was in the tennis matches played almost daily beneath his window.

In spite of this farce, Philip tried valiantly to act as his own man. Without consulting Olivares he appointed a new military commander. It was a bold stroke, but it proved of little consequence: the army suffered another crushing defeat before the Catalan city of Lérida. Philip, however, did not lose heart. He returned to Madrid in December 1642 to put together yet another army. In his absence, there had been a surprising development in the capital: Queen Isabel had been gathering around her a clique of noblemen highly critical of Olivares. Her most recent reason for detesting him was the legitimization of Don Juan, Philip's bastard son by the actress María Calderón. The Minister had encouraged the King to recognize the 13-year-old Don Juan, and now, of course, Isabel's own son, Prince Baltasar Carlos, had a rival.

In this maneuver Olivares apparently acted out of self-interest. His only daughter had died and he had no other legitimate children. He did have, however, an illegitimate son and, to the outrage of relatives who expected to inherit his titles and land, he had made this boy his heir. By pushing the King to follow suit and give official status to Don Juan, Olivares hoped to win approval of his own act. Instead he earned the hostility of the court and of the Queen. "My efforts and my boy's innocence," the angry Isabel is reported to have said, "must serve the King for eyes, for if he uses those of [Olivares] much longer my son will be reduced to a poor king of Castile instead of King of Spain." Isabel's role in the war effort—she had helped to raise funds for the King's expedition to Catalonia —had won her the respect of the Madrileños. Philip must have noticed, on his return to the capital, how warmly she was cheered as they rode together to the Buen Retiro.

The general dissatisfaction with Olivares, long in building, now reached a crescendo of hatred as rigorous new decrees drawn up by him went into effect. They demanded too much of a people who had already given as much as they could possibly be expected to give, including their blood. Among other things, the decrees called for further "voluntary" donations to finance the war, the seizure of all gold and silver vessels and utensils in the possession of the Church or individuals, and the imposition of a 7 per cent tax on real estate. If the smoldering resentment of the people and court was to be quelled, it was imperative to rid Spain of the man who had brought her to the brink of disaster. The Queen begged Philip to dismiss the Minister. Others he trusted ventured to urge the same course on him, unburdening themselves of such tales of woe that the painful truth began to sink in.

At last Philip acted. He wrote to Olivares that the leave he had more than once requested in the past was now granted: he could go. Olivares was dumfounded. He tried to argue the King into keeping him on, and his wife interceded with the Queen, but Philip's mind was made up. Dismissal proved the one blow that the overworked, overwrought Minister could not take. He retired to the country, sank into madness and died two years later. It was subsequently said of him that he was "a great man who knew how to make gigantic designs, but he lacked aptitude in the execution of them and felicity in the outcome."

Olivares' downfall, ironically, came at a time of special honors for Velázquez. The fact that Olivares had been the man to call him to court was either forgotten or conveniently overlooked. A few weeks before the Minister's dismissal, Velázquez was made a Gentleman of the Bedchamber. Five months later, in June 1643, he was appointed Assistant Superintendent of Works at a salary of 70 ducats a month. This new job promised to keep him extremely busy; it involved overseeing the King's various building projects, including the refurbishing of the Alcázar, the old palace in Madrid.

With Olivares' departure, Philip's fortunes seemed also to change for the better. Whatever personal anxiety it may have cost him to fire the man on whom he had leaned for more than 25 years, the resulting sense of release buoyed him into thinking that he could carry on alone. He promptly announced to his councilors his determination to take charge of the government. His only minister henceforth, he said, would be his wife, whose valor and wisdom were known to all. When the Madrileños heard this, they were overjoyed. "Our King is King at last" was supposed to have been their cry.

Morale began to improve, and an end to the war seemed in sight. Cardinal Richelieu had died two months before Olivares' dismissal, and Louis XIII four months afterward. This left the French Queen nominally in charge as co-regent for her five-year-old son, Louis XIV; she was none other than Philip's older sister Anne, and through all the long years of war she had never lost her sympathy for Spain.

But now Spanish pride asserted itself; the French had to be driven from the country before peace could be concluded. For a second time Philip prepared to take the field against the insurgent Catalans and the French.

The French forces had swept deep into Aragon and were within a few miles of Saragossa. At this critical juncture—June 1643—came black news from Flanders. A force of 20,000 men, put together at great expense, had been hopelessly crushed by the French at Rocroi. Spain's pretensions as a world military power were now as good as dead.

Philip nonetheless set out with his army for Aragon. Much of his earlier resolve had wilted, and he was casting about for someone new on whom he could lean. He had begun to entrust many of the details of government to Don Luís de Haro, a disaffected nephew of Olivares. As the King slowly made his way to the front, he stopped on July 10 at the Convent of the Immaculate Conception in Ágreda to meet Sister María, a nun famous for her holiness and wisdom. Sister María's influence on the King was to be enormous. During this first encounter, she exhorted him to put all his trust in God, to believe in himself and in his ability to bring about change. She reminded him of his duty as a Christian to lead a good and clean life—and to set an example for all his people to follow. The force of her personality was such that Philip felt himself uplifted, his will reinforced. Before leaving the convent, he made the nun promise to write to him—and pray for him.

Philip arrived in Saragossa in late July, this time without his usual retinue of high-living courtiers—a fact that gave the Saragossans increased confidence in his leadership. Soon he was in active correspondence with Sister María, and letters went back and forth almost weekly. In his first letter the King spoke so revealingly of himself that his own words are worth quoting: "Since the day that I was with you I have felt much encouraged by your promise to pray to God for me. . . . As I told you, I left Madrid lacking all human resources, and trusting only to divine help, which is the sole way to obtain what we desire. Our Lord has already begun to work in my favor . . . I have been able, though with infinite trouble and tardiness for want of money, to dispose my forces here so that we shall, I hope, start work with them this week. Although I beseech God and His most Holy Mother to succor and aid us, I trust very little in myself; for I have offended, and still offend very much, and I justly deserve the punishments and afflictions which I suffer. And so I appeal to you to fulfill your promise to me to clamor to God to guide my actions and my arms, to the end that the quietude of these realms may be secured, and peace reign throughout Christendom."

Sister María's counsel inspired Philip, and her prayers seemed to deliver him. His army began to do well. On December 3, 1643, the city of Monzon, some 20 miles inside Aragon, fell to the Spaniards. An elated Philip returned to Madrid to spend Christmas with his family. To demonstrate to all that he was a changed man, he bypassed the luxurious Buen Retiro and headed for the grim Alcázar. He spent his days there soberly, continuing his correspondence with Sister María. With motherly concern she urged him "to make yourself thoroughly versed in everything touching you." And perhaps taking into account his dependent personality, she recommended that he choose a competent adviser, thereby opening the door wider for Haro. Philip thanked the nun for her prayers and advice and mentioned that he was awaiting an event of great moment

—the arrival of the ships of the Silver Fleet from South America. "You may imagine what depends upon it for us," he wrote, "and although I hope that, in His Mercy, He will bring them safely, I want to urge you to help me by supplicating His Divine Majesty to do me this favor. It is true, I do not deserve it, but rather great punishment; but I have full confidence that He will not permit the total loss of this monarchy, and that He will continue the successes that He has begun to give us."

The Silver Fleet arrived safely, bringing five million ducats' worth of treasure for the King to use on the war, "and almost as much for private owners." Philip prepared to rejoin his army, and ordered Velázquez to accompany him. A large party set out for Aragon on February 6, 1644. In March came word that the Queen was pregnant again, followed soon after by the grim news that she had suffered a miscarriage and was ill. In spite of this blow, the King pressed on.

Before an attack on the French-occupied city of Lérida, Philip paused with his army at Fraga, a town on the border between Catalonia and Aragon. There he commanded Velázquez to paint him. An easel was built for the artist, and a window was cut through the wall of the ramshackle house in which he worked so as to give him enough light. Philip came to pose over a three-day period, dressed in a field uniform consisting of a red woolen coat trimmed with silver braid, a buff-colored elkskin vest and a black hat with red plumes. Each day new bundles of reeds would be spread upon the ground to keep the King's feet warm.

Despite the primitive conditions under which Velázquez was forced to work, he produced not only the portrait of the King *(page 104)* but another of the dwarf known as El Primo, "The Cousin" *(pages 126 and 127)*, who although stunted in body was intellectually gifted, and traveled with the royal entourage as a kind of secretary. Velázquez may have induced El Primo to sit for him in order to loosen up his hand for the more important task of portraying Philip. But if this was his motive, it did not prevent him from painting the dwarf as brilliantly and sympathetically as the King, though with a very different technique. In the portrait of Philip, the face is built up from almost transparent glazes, and flurries of quick strokes suggest the rich details of the royal uniform. El Primo's face and body, by contrast, are modeled with thick, broad strokes. He holds in his lap an enormous volume, with an inkwell and books at his feet; these emphasize his tiny proportions. His face is among the wisest and most intelligent ever painted by Velázquez, and his black, penetrating eyes—tinged by depression—speak of the disillusionment of the times.

Ten years had passed since Velázquez had painted the King for the Hall of Realms. The portrait at Fraga shows Philip changed. Gone is the old vanity. He has marshaled all his strength for one great effort. He has a firm grip on the royal baton and his face is set with determination —though he cannot quite conceal the weariness he must have been feeling in his heart. Soon after the painting was finished, Lérida fell to the Spaniards. The victory was to be only temporary, but Philip was hailed as a hero. Out of pride, he had the portrait crated and shipped to the Queen that she, too, might see him in his new role.

Toys of the King

The 17th Century Spanish court lived in a straitjacket of rigid protocol, and the members of the Royal Family were its most tightly fettered victims. They unbent only when they were hunting or playing with pets, particularly such human pets as dwarfs, half-wits and jesters. The fad of maintaining a retinue of clowns and human oddities had faded in other European courts, but it lingered—even flourished—in Madrid. Palace records of Philip IV's day list 110 of these retainers by name and refer to scores of others who trailed the King on his yearly circuit of the palaces, estates and hunting lodges that were scattered around his realm. The gloomy Habsburgs needed the spur of professional entertainment; besides relishing the antics of buffoons and the clumsiness of the retarded, they found a singular pleasure in the company of dwarfs. A king, wary of normal human contacts because so much depended on his personal favor, could pamper a dwarf without arousing the envy of the courtiers who were in constant attendance upon him during his peregrinations; a dwarf's life was irrelevant.

The artists who preceded Velázquez at the Spanish court painted dwarfs with a cold detachment that reflected the prevailing 16th and 17th Century attitude toward the handicapped. Velázquez, on the other hand, portrayed Philip IV's fools and dwarfs with warmth and understanding, conveying his own recognition that these unfortunate creatures were as human as their masters.

The jester Pablo de Valladolid strikes a pose in emulation of the actors in the Spanish theater, one of the King's favorite diversions, in this airy portrait by Velázquez. Detached from reality—only the points where his feet join his shadow are defined—the jester's figure floats in the magic, make-believe atmosphere of the theater.

Pablo de Valladolid, c. 1635

122

Philip IV as a Hunter, 1632-1633

Juan Bautista Martínez del Mazo, *The Stag Hunt at Aranjuez*, c. 1636

Velázquez painted the 28-year-old Philip IV
in a happy mood *(above)*, dressed for his favorite
sport, proud of his fine dog and flintlock. A
tireless hunter, Philip moved constantly from
the Sierras to the riverside town of Aranjuez in
pursuit of game. He seldom missed the spring
stag hunts at Aranjuez—events that combined
the charms of a circus and a slaughterhouse. At
these "meets," the deer—reserved for the royal
party—were rounded up by dogs and beaters,
driven down a long, narrow run and spitted by
swordsmen in front of a spectators' stand.
Velázquez' protégé and son-in-law Mazo painted
such a royal "hunt" in all its gory splendor
(left). In view of the Queen and her ladies, who
were seated on a stand erected above the end
of the deer run, Philip and his courtiers would
lunge at the frightened beasts; any that escaped
their thrusts were dispatched behind the stand.

Antonis Mor, *Estanislao*, 1560

Sánchez Coello, *Isabel Clara Eugenia with Madalena Ruíz*, c. 1580

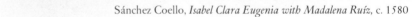

The portraits on these pages illustrate both the stiff, detailed style of late 16th and early 17th Century Spanish court painters and the contemporary attitude toward the court dwarfs, conveyable chattels who were shuttled from place to place at their masters' whims. Estanislao (*far left*) was a gift from the King of Poland to Philip II, who had him painted by the Flemish-born portraitist Antonis Mor.

Mor also executed the portrait at far right of the dwarf Estevanillo, about whose origins nothing is known. Mor's meticulous attention to the details of dress and to the huge hound and crouching ape he included in the portraits suggests that the artist had no deeper feeling for the dwarfs than for the animals. Mor's pupil, Sánchez Coello, followed his master's style in his rigid portrait of the

Rodrigo de Villandrando, *Philip IV and the Dwarf Soplillo*, c. 1618

Antonis Mor, *Court Dwarf Estevanillo*, 1563-1568

Infanta Isabel with her dwarf Madalena Ruíz. Every thread of the Infanta's magnificent gown and every hair of her rare South American marmosets are rendered with painstaking accuracy, but Madalena exists only as a foil to Isabel's noble beauty. When Rodrigo de Villandrando painted the teen-aged future Philip IV with his stunted playmate Soplillo—a present from the prince's Aunt Isabel in Flanders—the artist carried the convention of stiff posture and minute detail to its arid extreme.

Velázquez' approach differed radically; his style was loose and evocative and he painted the handicapped, like the royal family, with humanity. His pictures of dwarfs, buffoons and half-wits respect their dignity as human beings and delineate their individual personalities.

125

Don Diego de Acedo, "El Primo," 1644

In contrast to the portraits on the previous pages, Velázquez' painting of Don Diego de Acedo depicts a human being of vigorous intellect and cool assurance. Executed within days of the portrait of Philip IV in uniform *(page 104)*, the picture shows the dwarf while he was on campaign with his royal master. Don Diego sits on the ground among the tools of his profession: inkwell, quill, books and ledgers. For this was no human bauble; during his 25 years at court, Don Diego served in an important post as one of the King's secretaries.

The origins of most court fools and dwarfs are unknown, but Don Diego's nickname, El Primo (The Cousin), roused a dozen rumors linking him to great families. Although Don Diego's secret will remain forever his own, his face in Velázquez' superb portrait undeniably projects nobility of character.

Calabazas, 1637-1639

Velázquez posed the little cross-eyed jester known as Calabazas between a pair of gourds, for the nickname meant "gourd," or "empty head." The glass at the buffoon's feet may have been a comment on Calabazas' liking for drink, a desire generously indulged by the King. Besides the customary reward of tidbits and wine earned by entertainers who could raise a laugh at official banquets, Calabazas enjoyed a daily ration that included a fowl, fruit, three pounds of meat (eggs on days of abstinence), as well as the luxury of snow from the distant Sierras to cool his ample supply of wine. By recognizing Calabazas' human frailties, Velázquez made even more poignant his portrayal of helpless but hopeful dependency.

The frothy execution of Calabazas' lace collar contrasts markedly with the precision favored by earlier court painters. In fact, Velázquez' casual style in such details once cost him a commission; a lady refused her portrait because she felt that he had neglected her expensive laces.

Don Sebastian de Morra, mid-1640s

Don Sebastian de Morra, a dwarf who was clearly never resigned to his fate, glares defiantly at the world from the prison of his body. As always recording the man within, Velázquez painted him from an angle that accentuates both his handicap and his obvious resentment. Above Don Sebastian's foreshortened, doll-like body and legs, his head and shoulders loom with the dark power of a fierce commander. He shows none of the aristocratic reserve of his fellow dwarf, El Primo; his somber pride suggests a soldier's temperament, raging against a world in which not even his own body was his to command. In 1643 Philip IV requisitioned Don Sebastian, like a toy tin soldier, from the entourage of his younger brother Fernando, then stationed in Flanders. The dwarf was shipped off to Madrid to attend the heir-apparent to the throne, Prince Baltasar Carlos. Don Sebastian must have earned his young master's affection, for Baltasar Carlos bequeathed several swords and daggers to the dwarf.

131

Francisco Lezcano, 1643-1645

Velázquez' painting of the cretinous dwarf Francisco Lezcano is the most moving of his extraordinary portraits of the mental and physical cripples who served the pleasure of the Spanish court. Other playthings like him were handsomely dressed, but this boy is as rumpled as a neglected two-year-old; he was, in fact, at least 14 at the time he sat for the artist. His pudgy hands fumble with a pack of cards—perhaps a fortunetelling tarot pack, in which the fool is an important card—and his outsize head lolls weakly to one side. Velázquez painted Francisco so accurately that present-day physicians can recognize the cause of his stunted development: he suffered from a thyroid deficiency. But Velázquez' genius was also compassionate; he probed beyond the unfortunate child's shadowed mind to the embryonic personality that glimmers in Francisco's naïve half-smile.

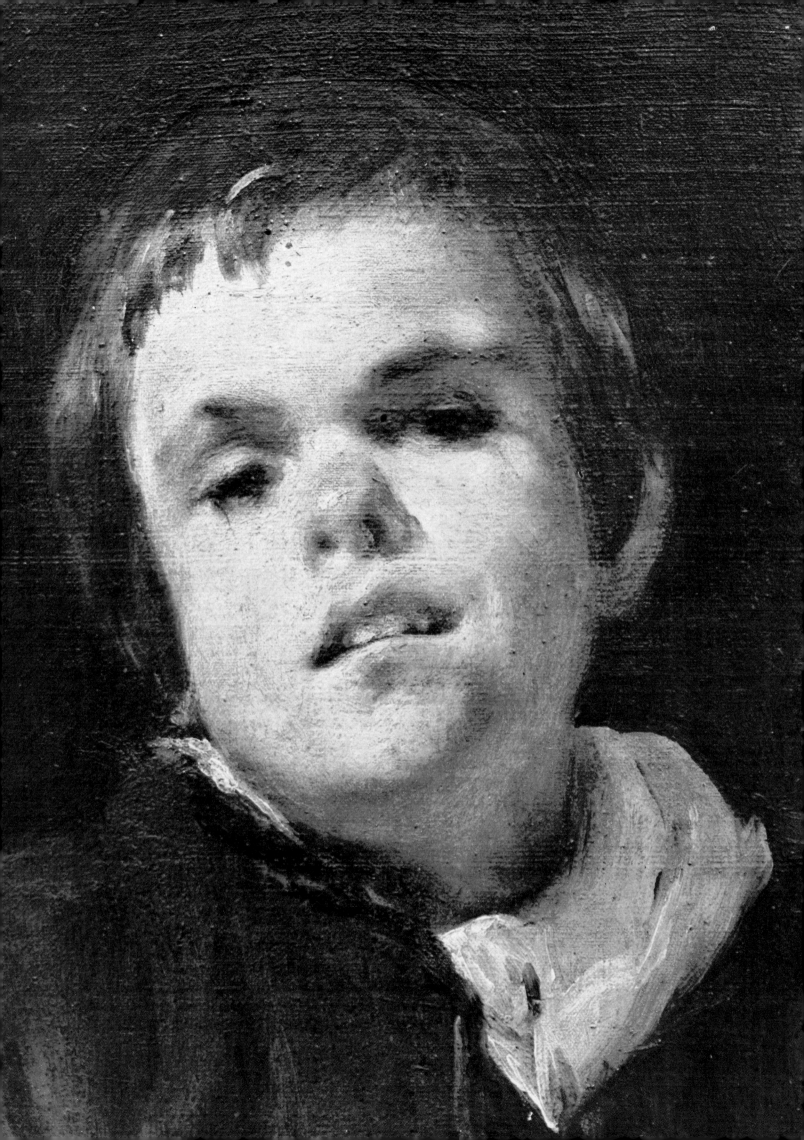

VI

The Spain
of Many Sorrows

A major characteristic of Velázquez' art is its serenity. There is a cool, almost classical order to his paintings. Looking at his work, it is sometimes hard to believe that all was not right with his world. His pictures rarely betray the strife of the period, the worsening situation of Spain, the anxieties of King and people. Death stalked the court; the royal mausoleum *(left)* being completed in the Escorial was to be useful far sooner than anyone anticipated. Yet almost none of the tragedy of the times shows in Velázquez' work. Instead we see in it a display of pride—pride as a whole way of being. Velázquez' ability to rise above his times, to paint and to go on painting in that quietly forceful manner of his, has something to say about the function of such pride in 17th Century Spain. The need for pride was great—as a defense against reality.

Spain's plight grew more desperate as time wore on. Even events that seemingly went well often turned out to be disasters, and Philip, whose mood could affect all around him, became increasingly pessimistic. The victory over the French invaders at Lérida in August 1644 had ushered in a period seemingly filled with possibilities for him and for Spain. A little more resolve, a little more effort, and Spain's fortunes might have improved. But Philip was incapable of sustaining resolve for long. Soon after the recapture of Lérida, he received the first of several blows that would leave him a shattered man, unable to lead effectively.

While Philip and Velázquez were still in the field, word came that the Queen had fallen gravely ill. Philip set off in haste, but not even fresh relays of mules could get his coach back to Madrid in time. Isabel's condition rapidly deteriorated. She was bled, and the body of Isidore the Plowman, Madrid's patron saint, was brought to her room with other relics and holy objects in the hope of producing a miraculous cure. The entire capital offered prayers on her behalf. But her malady—which today would be diagnosed as diphtheria—resisted treatment (such as it was), and it became clear that she was dying. She called for her children, Baltasar Carlos and María Teresa, to say a last farewell, but made them stand far from her bed lest she infect them. "There are plenty of Queens for Spain," she said, "but Princes and Princesses are rare." The next day, October 6,

135

1644, Isabel died—and thus fell away one of the King's main supports.

The news was broken to Philip on the road to Madrid. "I find myself in the most oppressed state of sorrow possible," he wrote to his new confidante, Sister María, "for I have lost in one person everything that can be lost in this world; and if I did not know, according to the faith that I profess, that the Lord disposes for us of what is best, I do not know what would become of me." The King secluded himself in his hunting lodge; then, following tradition, he took up residence in the hermitage of San Gerónimo, adjacent to the Buen Retiro, for the official mourning period. In the meantime the body of the Queen, dressed in the robes of a Franciscan nun, was borne in a stately procession across the rocky plain between Madrid and the Escorial and entombed with great pomp in the monastery-palace.

With Sister María's encouragement Philip tried to recover from his shock and in the spring of 1645 he resumed active direction of the campaign against the French. This time he took the 15-year-old Baltasar Carlos with him, fully aware of the risks involved. He explained to the nun: "I have wanted the Prince to begin to learn what will fall upon him after my days are done; and so, though alone, I have brought him with me, and have consigned his health to the hands of God, trusting in His mercy to guard him, and to guide all his actions to His greater service."

Still, Philip's black mood persisted. And as his armies suffered one reverse after another, he became more than ever convinced that God was punishing him for past sins. Yet he held out the hope, which he confided to Sister María, that the Lord, in looking down on the Spanish realms, "which are so pure in their Catholic faith, will not allow us to be ruined utterly, and grant us a good peace." Encouraged by the knowledge that Sister María and the nuns of her convent were praying for him seven times a day, Philip determined to court heavenly favor by continuing to fight his weaknesses.

The King spent the summer of 1645 with the Prince in Saragossa, directing the campaign from a safe distance, and in the fall he persuaded the Aragonese to swear allegiance to Baltasar Carlos as their future king. Apparently Velázquez did not accompany Philip to Saragossa. Records of the court for that year indicate that he was busy in Madrid at least part of the time, and they also suggest that he may have been going through a period of considerable personal trial. A dispute had arisen over his handling of a project in the Alcázar—the construction of an alcove for which he had primary responsibility as Assistant Superintendent of Works. The architect had sent word to the King that Velázquez was departing from the plans, and in doing so would weaken the structure. Philip's reply was succinct: "Diego Velázquez, you are a subject, and as such, you shall obey." Evidently this rebuke upset Velázquez a great deal, and he responded by petitioning Philip for the money due him as Assistant Superintendent. He had reason to be irked; he had not received his salary for more than two years. The King then directed that Velázquez be paid promptly.

After spending the winter in Madrid, Philip and Baltasar Carlos again set out for the front as the war's activities resumed in the spring of 1646.

Going by way of Pamplona in the north, where the Prince was to receive an oath of loyalty from the people of Navarre, they stopped briefly at Ágreda. There Philip showed off his son to Sister María. The nun found the boy intelligent and beautifully behaved, and she made a point of telling this to the proud father. But the King's pleasure at her response soon vanished. At Pamplona the young Prince contracted malaria. Although the Aragonese begged the King to come to direct the campaign, Philip refused to leave his son's bedside and waited until they could travel together. When at last they arrived in Saragossa, after a two-month delay, Philip learned of the death of his sister Doña María, whom years before he had sent to marry King Ferdinand of Hungary, now Holy Roman Emperor. This blow, coming so soon after his son's illness, left Philip badly shaken, and he once again wrote beseechingly to Sister María: "If I did not recognize that my troubles are sent by God, as warnings for me to prepare my own salvation, I could hardly tolerate them. Help me, Sister María, to pray to Him; for my strength is small, and I fear my weakness."

The death of his sister set Philip to thinking about the future in another way. The Emperor was of course not only Philip's brother-in-law, but his cousin. Both were Habsburgs, related several times over through intermarriages of the Spanish and Austrian branches of the family. Cooperation between the two branches had long been a fundamental part of Philip's foreign policy, and it was toward this end that he had married off his sister to Ferdinand. Now, with her death, he sought to replace that broken family tie with another, proposing that the 16-year-old Baltasar Carlos marry Ferdinand's 11-year-old daughter, Mariana. Philip saw arising from such a union "very beneficial effects to the Catholic religion," as he wrote Sister María, perhaps hoping that she would pass the word along to God.

The Prince himself seemed pleased over the prospect of the marriage. He too was in correspondence with Sister María, and he poured out his feelings to her in a boyish letter dated July 20, 1646: "Two or three days ago my father gave me a letter from you congratulating me on the marriage he has made for me with the Archduchess Mariana. I am the most pleased in the world at the idea of marriage, especially with my cousin, who was the one I wished for ever since I had use of my reason; and it seems impossible to me that I could have come across any other woman so much to my taste. So I hope His Divine Majesty will let us be very happily married, which is all I can hope for. I ask you to pray for this."

But the Prince's hopes and the King's planning came to no avail. Sometimes it almost seemed that Philip was cursed—that he was indeed being punished for his sins. In Saragossa in October the Prince became ill, suffering a high fever and intense pain. In great agitation Philip wrote Sister María: "I do cry now to the divine mercy of our Lord, and the intercession of His Holy Mother; and I beseech you to help with all your strength." A few days afterward he wrote again: "I have lost my only son, and such a son, as you know he was."

The King was in torment. In the space of two years he had lost his wife, his sister and now his beloved son Baltasar Carlos. Spain's enemies

Sister María de Jesús, to whom Philip IV turned for spiritual guidance, was the subject of many fanciful stories that were widely believed in her time. Above, in the frontispiece of a book of her adventures by a Franciscan priest, she appears preaching to Indians in New Mexico—an endeavor she undertook, according to the padre, while simultaneously attending to her duties in Spain. This was supposedly possible because the nun was transported to America by a covey of angels. Sister María modestly confessed that the story was exaggerated and that perhaps an angel had impersonated her.

Velázquez' son-in-law, Martínez del Mazo, began painting this view of Saragossa while King Philip was directing the war against the French from that northern Spanish city. Through Velázquez' influence, Mazo had been appointed drawing master to Philip's son Prince Baltasar Carlos, who was traveling with his father. The young prince is said to have selected the site where Mazo set up his canvas, on the bank of the Ebro, midway between the main bridges leading to the city. Tragically, the 17-year-old Prince died of smallpox in Saragossa while Mazo was at work on the painting; it was finished in 1647, a year after Baltasar Carlos' death, at Philip's command.

pressed his dominions everywhere—in Portugal, Catalonia, Italy, Flanders. The royal treasury was nearly empty. Where was a sign that Sister María's prayers were being heard? If Spain was being denied help because of the gravity of his sins, if God was punishing him by taking away one by one those he loved, what was the use of trying to be good? Nonetheless, Philip resolved to meet his dynastic obligations. He decided to remarry, in the hope of producing another male heir, and the bride he chose was Baltasar Carlos' betrothed, the politically valuable Mariana of Austria—his own niece. But before the marriage could take place, funds for it had to be dug up from somewhere, and money was in short supply in both houses of the Habsburgs. Nearly three years were to elapse before the King, at 44, and the Princess, at 15, became man and wife. In the interim Philip began to feel the tug of all the old weaknesses, the compulsions that surged up from within—and to these he eventually succumbed. His renewed licentiousness became common knowledge. One courtier dared write in his diary: "God save us from him who is liberal

to vice and stingy to virtue, for the only people now who are comfortable and placed aloft are concubines and the women who look after them, low and common women, and those men who have been base enough to marry them."

Sister María was so agitated over what she heard and surmised that she wrote to Philip on November 15, 1647, and gave him a thorough talking-to: "My Lord, no man can be truly a king who is not ruler of himself, controlling and having complete mastery over his desires and passions; because if they hold dominion over him, then he is not a king but their slave. It is by crushing them down and refusing to be ruled by them that the king's heart is put in the hand of the Lord, and the purpose of doing that is to free the king from being dogged by punishments he has deserved and from continual anxiety about obtaining salvation. Of course, God does not hold the king's heart in His hand only to defend and refresh it. The hand of God is strong and presses hard, which is why God said, 'Whom I love, I correct.' Though all human hearts need such correction, most of all do the hearts of kings in order that their wealth and magnificence in this vale of tears do not lead them into sin."

Sister María put pressure upon Philip to reform not only himself, but his realm. Her methods were varied. From the first meeting of nun and King she had been urging him to "prohibit the wearing of immodest clothes because they corrupt morals." After the Queen's death, she bolstered her plea with a report that she had seen a vision of Isabel in a dress of flames, suffering the tortures of the damned for the vain pleasures of her earthly existence. Taking the war into account, she boldly informed Philip that she "would promise God, that if we are granted respite there shall be a general reform in Spain and an improvement in the lives of one and all of us."

Philip was left with no alternative but to act. He asked his councilors and bishops to investigate the scandals tainting his country and recommend ways of combating them. He took some preliminary steps of his own, beginning where Isabel, moved by conscience, had left off. Shortly before her death, she had placed restrictions on the theater, once her great passion. By her command plays were to deal only with historical or religious themes, and players were forbidden the ostentation of costumes of gold cloth. Actresses had to be married, and none might receive a backstage visit from the same gentleman more than twice. Philip closed all theaters. In addition, he ordered his subjects to wear modest dress, and the penalties for crimes were increased. Outwardly, at least, Madrid became the soberest of cities. Still Sister María was not satisfied.

She reported that she had seen three apparitions of Baltasar Carlos. He spoke, she said, of all the many evils afflicting Spain, so numerous and so dreadful that even if given the chance to return to life, he would refuse it. God had rescued him from the clutches of the devil just in time, and now he feared that his sister, María Teresa, though only eight, might be similarly endangered. He urged that she be brought up in the fear of the Lord. On his most recent appearance, Sister María said, Baltasar Carlos had announced that God had entrusted her with the divine responsibility of promoting the King's best interests.

With this mandate she lost no time in pointing out to Philip the dangers —political as well as moral—that surrounded him. Many of the men closest to the throne were his enemies, she declared, cheats who had achieved their eminence through flattery and other false means, while many others who could help the King were kept away. In the name of Baltasar Carlos, she implored Philip to remove his evil councilors, and she warned of the dangers of putting too much trust—and therefore too much power —in the hands of any individual. God, she let it be known, disapproved of all the jockeying for position that went on in the palace hierarchy.

Philip was not entirely persuaded by the nun's argument. In his reply he reminded her that a monarch had to delegate authority; it would not befit his station if he wandered from office to office to see to the enforcement of his decrees. If, Philip added, he had committed the error in his early years of depending too much on one person, he had made an effort since then to correct his mistakes. He could not, however, do without a First Minister; besides, he had full confidence in the man who now performed the duties of that office, Don Luís de Haro, his friend since childhood. He assured the nun: "I, Sister María, do not shirk any form of work, and, as all can witness, I am more or less continually seated in this chair with my papers before me and my pen in my hand." He added that he was aware of the struggle for power constantly being waged in the palace and of the reprehensible methods employed by those who sought it. But, he said, "it will require the help of God to get rid of these jealous rivalries at Court, for they spring from human weakness and are characteristic of all courts at all times, and, without God's help, I shall find it hard to remedy an ill so deeply engrained in the ambitious nature of most men."

There was certainly no shortage at court of petty rivalries; Velázquez himself became involved in one at the very time the King wrote of them. His seniority as a Gentleman of the Bedchamber was challenged by another Gentleman of the Bedchamber. The issue boiled down to the validity of the oaths each had taken upon assumption of office. After careful inquiry, the matter was resolved in Velázquez' favor, but still another problem arose. Early in 1647 he had become the supervisor and paymaster of a major project, the construction of a new gallery in the Alcázar, the so-called Octagonal Room. The job, an important one that had been taken from the Superintendent and given to Velázquez, promised additional income. But as before when Velázquez had accepted and discharged large responsibilities, he found himself unpaid. In May he filed a petition saying that he felt discrimination—he had not received wages since 1645, although others had. Once again promises were made that he would be paid, but these too may have proved ephemeral; the government declared itself bankrupt in October 1647.

Despite his heavy official work load, Velázquez did manage to produce several important works around this time—but apparently for private collectors, not for the harassed King. *Venus at Her Mirror (pages 150-151)* is believed to be one of these. It shows the goddess lying naked on a divan, her back turned to the viewer. She is all soft pinkness and gentle curves as she stares approvingly at herself in the mirror held by a plump Cupid. Her reflection is blurred—but not so blurred that her features cannot be made out in the glass. They are very much like those of Mary in *The Coronation of the Virgin,* a work Velázquez is thought to have executed for Queen Isabel before her death in 1644. Who was the model? One clue to her identity may lie in the fact that a popular Spanish actress had achieved a certain notoriety by using black sheets on her bed; Velázquez' Venus shares her idiosyncrasy. All that is certain about this sensuous painting is that it once belonged to the Marquis of Eliche, son of Haro, the First Minister, and owner of at least three other works by Velázquez.

Another painting that Velázquez is believed to have executed for a private collector before 1648 is *The Fable of Arachne,* long known as *The Spinners (pages 152-155).* Not until fairly recently was the painting's original title rediscovered and its mythological subject—a weaving contest between a girl called Arachne and the Greek goddess Pallas Athena —ascertained. Formerly the painting was thought to be simply a genre scene, a view of the tapestry workrooms in the royal palace, and it can still be appreciated on that level alone. Several women are busy at various chores in the foreground—one is spinning, another is picking up fluffs of wool, another is dexterously winding a ball of yarn. The atmosphere is dense, warm, shadowy; a cat with its paws tucked under its body drowses on the floor. The paint itself is dense—almost woolly—as though it had been swept onto the canvas with thick brushes. The colors are for the most part dark, earthy. The only really bright spot is an alcove filled with blinding sunshine at the rear of the room. In it may be seen several other women, including one in armor, against a tapestry backdrop based on a prize picture in the royal collection, Titian's large canvas, *The Rape of Europa*.

The painting is a transcendent example of Velázquez' naturalism—an attempt to render on canvas what his eye saw. As virtually all of his pictures show, he was interested in the real world, even when his subjects were mythological or religious. In his early *bodegones* he was preoccupied with the look and feel of a few carefully chosen objects, and he tended to render these in sharp focus. But he eventually realized that this is not the way things are seen, and more and more he let his eye guide his brush. Having observed that the eye sees sharply only the object it is focused on, he began to paint, as it were, *in* and *out* of focus. The faces on which he was concentrating are usually sharply defined in his portraits, and the costumes are not.

By painting scenes as he saw them, Velázquez achieved a freshness and spontaneity that give canvases like *The Fable of Arachne* and *Venus at Her Mirror* their timeless look. But to many literal-minded people their sketchy passages—the loosely rendered Cupid in *Venus at Her Mirror,* for instance—provide evidence that these paintings are unfinished. Yet surely Velázquez was only following his perceptions here. Cupid kneels off to one side and in the background, at the edge of the field of vision. If we had our gaze fixed on the recumbent model, as Velázquez did, we would have seen Cupid's face as Velázquez painted it—fuzzily.

In *Arachne* Velázquez went further and rendered the entire scene as if taken in at a glance. It is possible to imagine him coming in from outdoors, and waiting for his eyes to adjust to the darkness of the room. In painting this moment, he substituted optical truth for finicky detail. Thus he approximated reality more closely than he could have by laying on details. But what looks so casual, so uncontrived, could have been achieved only as the result of intensive observation. He even sought in *Arachne* to capture motion in paint. The spinning wheel is a blur of pigment, and the fluttering fingers of Arachne winding yarn are seen in successive positions at the same time.

It is largely because of this naturalism that the mythological content of *The Fable of Arachne* went so long unnoticed. In the myth, as told by the Roman poet Ovid in his *Metamorphoses,* Arachne dared boast to admirers that her weaving skills were superior to those of Pallas Athena, goddess of arts and crafts. When Athena heard of this, she disguised herself as an old woman and scolded Arachne for her audacity. But Arachne merely repeated her claim, whereupon Athena threw off her disguise, revealed

In the midst of war and depression, upheaval at court and his own personal troubles, the middle-aged Velázquez executed this chalk study for a portrait of Cardinal Borja, the Primate of Spain. Gaspar de Borja y Velasco was a harsh and ascetic man, a member of the Borgia family that was powerful throughout Europe. Despite his well-known miserliness, Borja offered to pay for the finished portrait. But Velázquez refused money and accepted instead an elaborate dressing gown and some silver ornaments as recompense. This is one of the few drawings Velázquez is known to have done; apparently he preferred to work directly on canvas rather than from studies like this one.

herself in armor and challenged Arachne to a weaving contest. After the wool had been spun, Athena wove six tapestries depicting the fate that befell mortals who dared defy the gods, while the bold Arachne chose for her theme the subjection of the gods to man's will. Arachne lost, and to punish the girl, Athena turned her into a spider (which is what *arachne* means in Greek).

Velázquez showed two episodes of the myth in his painting, blending them cleverly into the context of a single image—a kind of play within a play. The scene at the back of the workshop—in the well-lighted alcove —shows the confrontation between Arachne and Athena, who has just thrown off her disguise. The scene in the foreground depicts part of the actual contest between the two. Athena is presumed to be the spinner, and Arachne the girl winding wool with her back turned. Who the other women might be is a question much debated by scholars. The three in the alcove may represent admirers of Arachne's skill, or they may stand for muses, perhaps architecture, music and sculpture. Arachne herself may represent painting, for Velázquez was probably familiar with a late 16th Century Spanish interpretation of Ovid's tale. This held that it was a parable commenting on the bitterness that would be felt by an artist whose work had been unjustly criticized. Perhaps Velázquez was alluding in his painting to some personal disappointment, such as the dispute in 1645 over his handling of the plans for the alcove in the Alcázar.

After Velázquez was put in charge of the construction of the Octagonal Room, his prestige at court reached new heights. The fact that he, rather than the Superintendent of Buildings, had won the job suggests that he had powerful friends close to the King—perhaps the Marquis of Eliche and his father, Haro. In the fall of 1648 Philip announced that he wanted to set up a new picture gallery and asked Velázquez to choose the artists to be represented there. Velázquez took immediate advantage of the situation to promote a scheme of his own. He saw no reason, he said, why the King should have pictures "like those anybody can have." He suggested that Philip grant him leave to travel again to Italy, this time "to search for and purchase the best pictures to be found"—paintings by Titian, Veronese, Raphael and others—as well as antique statues or casts.

Almost two decades had passed since Velázquez had been to Italy. No doubt he had been dreaming of the day when he might return. Given the unsettled circumstances in Spain in the 1640s, it must have seemed a matter of going now or never. Who could tell what the future would bring? Plague had swept through Castile and Valencia and into Andalusia, where it killed half the population of Seville. Political unrest rumbled throughout the realm. A revolt in Spanish Naples was put down in 1648; a conspiracy in Aragon was quashed. Worse, from the long-range view, Spain's Austrian ally, the Holy Roman Emperor, took the momentous step in 1648 of signing a separate peace treaty with the French at Westphalia. From now on Spain would have to fight France unaided. Philip was despondent: "I am left out and have to face all my enemies alone." The one bright spot was the peace accord reached with the Dutch at Münster after 80 years of intermittent strife. At least Spain would now be free of this terrible drain on its resources. Although the international situation was still uneasy, the King approved Velázquez' trip and arrangements were promptly made.

The painter was given 2,000 ducats for traveling expenses, and "the carriage due him because of his position." He elected to take with him an assistant, Juan de Pareja. Together they set sail from Málaga late in January 1649, traveling with a party of noblemen delegated to bring Philip's bride-to-be, the young Mariana, back to Spain. Arriving in Genoa in early March, Velázquez headed straight for Venice. Although 20 years had elapsed since his first visit there, the atmosphere was apparently still as openly hostile to Spaniards as it had been in 1629, and the greatest tact was required to get people to show Velázquez their paintings. The artist did, however, purchase several Tintorettos and Veronese's glorious *Venus and Adonis.*

From Venice Velázquez set off for Rome, making brief courtesy calls en route. At Modena the Duke whose portrait he had executed in 1638 made him promise to pay a return visit; at Bologna the Count of Siena and other dignitaries rode out in their coaches to welcome him, and the count put him up in his palace. Increasingly, Velázquez must have felt himself a personage—presumably he was receiving all these honors because of his status as a gentleman of Philip IV's court, not solely because of his artistic reputation.

He could not have picked a better time to be in Italy. Rome was preparing for the Jubilee celebration of 1650, which had been proclaimed by Pope Innocent X. Some 700,000 pilgrims would visit the Eternal City before the year was over—among them many of the great painters, architects and sculptors of Europe. Here Velázquez probably met the French master of classical painting, Poussin, and Bernini, the pioneer exponent of the baroque style.

But before Velázquez could settle down in Rome, he had first to go to Naples to collect the rest of his travel money from Philip's viceroy there. He took advantage of his visit to have casts made of antique sculptures for shipment back to Spain, and he may have called on his countryman, Ribera. As soon as he had attended to his business, he returned to Rome —there to remain for more than a year. His excitement must have run high. He was received by some of the city's leading citizens and patrons of the arts.

Rome seemed to unleash in Velázquez a burst of creative energy. In 17 or 18 months he painted at least 10 portraits and began several others. Five of the finished portraits survive: they are of Innocent X *(pages 158 and 159)*; the Pope's barber, who bore the illustrious name Michelangelo; Cardinal Astalli, the Pope's adopted nephew; Camillo Massimo, the Papal Chamberlain; and Juan de Pareja, Velázquez' assistant. He painted these, according to his early biographer Palomino, "with long-handled brushes, in Titian's vigorous manner." By using long-handled brushes, Velázquez could paint at some distance from his canvas without having to step back from his easel to gauge his effects and interrupt his creative flow. This technique would also have given him greater mobility and lent the pictures a sense of spontaneity. Certainly the vitality of his work was much admired by his fellow painters. "Superiority," wrote one, "consists in doing much with a few brushstrokes, freely executed so that the studied effect may appear spontaneous. This admirable method Diego Velázquez is now making famous, for with subtle skill, with a few strokes, he shows how much freedom of touch, and a rapid execution can accomplish."

As the art center of 17th Century Europe, Rome offered Velázquez the chance of a lifetime to show off his talent, and he lost little time in doing so. He became a member of the painters' guild in January 1650, and a few weeks later was admitted to a confederation of artists called the *Virtuosi al Pantheon,* a group that every March held a prestigious exhibition at the Pantheon. What won him almost instant recognition was the portrait of Pareja. He did it as a kind of warm-up for his portrait of the Pope, but apparently also with an eye to the Pantheon show, where it was hung with works by fellow artists and great masters of the past. The portrait may have earned Velázquez contemporary acclaim, but certainly nothing like the accolade it received in 1971, when it was sold to the Metropolitan Museum of Art for a record-breaking $5,544,000. The painting is boldly executed, and Pareja seems alive in it, his eyebrows arched, his eyes alert. Many writers on Velázquez have referred to Pareja as his slave—presumably because Pareja was of Moorish ancestry—but one look at the painting is convincing evidence that a man as proud as this must have been free in spirit, if not in law.

Velázquez knew Pareja well, and this doubtless contributed to the spirit with which the painting was executed. The painter's achievement in portraying the Pope is even more remarkable. He hardly knew Innocent X. As a cardinal, the Pope had served as Papal Nuncio to the Spanish court from 1626 to 1630, and Velázquez may have observed him there, but his memory of the prelate would by this time have dimmed. Velázquez was probably granted only a few sittings with the busy Pope, but they were enough; for years the artist had been used to working quickly, painting the faces of his subjects from life and filling in the clothing and other details later.

Although Innocent was in his late seventies when Velázquez painted him, he looks much younger than his years. He wears a stern expression. His eyes, as one critic has noted, do not just stare out at the viewer: they scrutinize. They are eyes that take in everything. The mouth is broad, coarse, tightly shut. A scraggly mustache covers part of the upper lip. There is a gleam—perhaps of sweat—on the forehead and nose, and the skin has a reddish cast from the blood beneath it. Were it not for his papal robes, Innocent might be mistaken for a temporal ruler.

Innocent had a reputation for prudence, integrity and industry—as well as cheerfulness. His coat of arms showed the dove of peace carrying an olive branch in its beak, and in politics he walked, as he said, a silken thread between France and Spain, trying not to become involved in the affairs of either. This was no easy thing to do. The combination of his massive papal responsibilities and the problems of his own household, which was dominated by his ambitious, widowed sister-in-law, Olimpia Maldachini, made him increasingly moody, subject at times to fits of violence.

All the contradictions of the man are present in Velázquez' painting: the strength and the weakness, the beneficence and the bite. The right hand seems almost to twitch with nervous energy. When the Pope first saw the portrait, he is reported to have said, somewhat ambiguously, *"Troppo vero"*—'Too true." But he was not displeased. He offered Velázquez money, which the artist refused, proudly saying that his king paid him well enough. Velázquez, however, did take advantage of the situation to mention that he wanted to become a member of one of the three Spanish military-religious orders. The hint was not lost upon Innocent, who ordered the Papal Nuncio in Spain to promote Velázquez' cause at the Spanish court. As a further token of appreciation for the por-

Donna Olimpia Maldachini, the widowed sister-in-law of Pope Innocent X, dominated the Vatican and the Papal States to such an extent that foreign envoys paid court to her before they saw the Pontiff. Some cardinals even kept her portrait in their apartments, as if she were a sovereign. Pressured by others who were annoyed by her assumption of power, Innocent exiled her for two years but brought her back when he found he could not run his household without her. Velázquez painted her, but the work is lost. The bust above was made by Alessandro Algardi, the Pope's favorite sculptor.

DORIA GALLERY, ROME

trait, Innocent sent Velázquez a gold chain and medallion bearing a relief of his head, which the artist counted among his more valuable possessions. The portrait was equally appreciated outside the papal chambers; it amazed Rome, and was "copied by all as a study, and admired as a miracle." No fewer than 13 copies are extant today.

Although elated by his Roman successes, Velázquez did not neglect his mission, the purchase of paintings and sculptures for the King's collection. A Spanish cardinal at the papal court, however, took a dim view of Velázquez' activities, and in a letter home called them a swindle. We do not know the reason for this accusation; perhaps Velázquez was once again the victim of petty court jealousies. But it may have prompted Philip to begin clamoring for his painter's return. Early in February 1650 the King wrote to the Spanish Ambassador in Rome: "I have seen your letter of November sixth of last year in which you give me an account of Velázquez' work on the assignments entrusted to him, and since you know his phlegmatic temperament, it would be well for you to see that he does not exercise it but hastens the conclusion of the work and his departure as much as possible." The King wanted Velázquez to leave Italy by the end of May or the beginning of June, and to bring with him the Italian frescoist, Pietro da Cortona, who was to help decorate the Alcázar. To make sure that Velázquez would find "neither excuse, nor pretext" for staying longer in Italy, Philip ordered his viceroy in Naples to provide the artist only the funds for his passage home. In addition, Philip ordered that Velázquez be forbidden to make the trip by land for fear that he might linger on the way, "the more so because of his nature." Apparently Velázquez had hoped to visit Paris in spite of the war and already had a visa for the journey.

Souvenir gold medallions were struck in Rome in 1650, when Pope Innocent X declared a Jubilee, or Holy Year. Innocent gave one of the medals on a gold chain to Velázquez after he had painted the Pope's portrait. Innocent's profile in relief on the medal makes him look rather a bland character; it seems small wonder that he was cowed by his dominating sister-in-law.

VATICAN MEDAL COLLECTION

The suggestion that Velázquez was dilatory seems deserved in this instance. He completely disregarded the King's order on the excuse that Cortona could not go with him to Spain. He launched a search for another frescoist—and managed to postpone his departure by four or five months, making it almost a year since Philip had first begun to pressure him to come home. During this time he visited Venice, where he bought paintings for the royal collection, and stopped at Modena to see the Duke again, perhaps in the hope of undertaking some work for him. The Duke was away, and Velázquez found himself being treated with suspicion by the ducal secretary, who apparently shared the prevalent Italian feeling that Spaniards were seldom up to any good. The secretary refused to show Velázquez the Duke's fine picture gallery and shunted him off, instead, to the nearby Palazzo Sassuolo, where he pointed out the frescoes, secure in the knowledge that these could not be removed from the walls and spirited away.

It is easy to understand why Velázquez was reluctant to leave Italy. He had been free to paint whatever and whomever he pleased. Moreover, he had won the approbation of his fellow artists, and he had been much stimulated by their company. But as painter to the King he could not stay away forever. When he no longer had any excuse for further delay, he set out with what could only have been a heavy heart for Spain —the Spain of many sorrows.

A Daring Maturity

In a lifetime of successes, Velázquez might have repeated endlessly what he had already done so masterfully. But he was not the kind of painter who allowed his art to hover at dead center. His self-confidence and curious eye led him constantly down new trails, and he dared to paint subjects others shied away from. While he continued to paint portraits with consummate skill and understanding *(right)*, he was not afraid to risk offending convention in a society that was at least publicly prudish by producing a portrait of a naked Venus. He experimented with technique, offering innovations inspired by personal observation of the way things are seen. Velázquez realized, for example, that quickly moving fingers and the turning spokes of a spinning wheel appear to the eye as indistinct forms, as do objects on which the eye is not directly focused. And he painted them that way. By employing such meticulous observations, he rose to even greater heights as a portraitist. In Rome, in 1650, he painted Pope Innocent X, focusing so directly upon the papal features, while leaving hands and robe fuzzily outlined, that the Pontiff seems about to spring from his chair. But there is more than technique to be found in this masterly and insightful portrait. It was so frank a revelation of character that Velázquez' contemporaries were astounded, and Innocent himself hinted that the painter had dared to tell more about him than he wanted known.

An unknown lady, perhaps a member of the artist's family, sat for this Velázquez portrait. The paint is spread thinly, as in many of his later works, projecting a gossamer beauty without sacrificing reality. Velázquez also added a surprise touch: a mysterious red dot of paint below the white bow of the dress, which, like a small flame, warms all the other colors of the canvas.

Lady with a Fan, 1632-1635

Because of the influence of the Church and the Inquisition and a general national obsession with the rectitude of women, the painters of Spain have produced relatively few female nudes. Yet Velázquez' *Venus at Her Mirror,* probably painted before his trip to Italy in 1648, is one of the most beautiful any country can boast. The other famous nude in Spanish art, Goya's *Naked Maja,* was inspired by this painting, and there has been endless speculation about the identities of the models in both works. One clue to the identity of Velázquez' nude may be in the setting. He painted her recumbent on what appear to be black taffeta sheets; at the time in Spain there was an actress who had a notorious preference for this particular item of bedroom décor. Whoever the lady was, Velázquez gave her the grace of a goddess; she reclines languidly, supremely confident of her charms.

In our own time, the painting has suffered shabby treatment. A recent cleaning stripped off sections of paint, exposing areas that Velázquez had deliberately painted over. But the worst affront to the lovely *Venus* occurred at London's National Gallery in 1914, when a militant suffragette attacked it with a small hatchet that she had hidden in her muff. She hacked at the painting angrily in an irrational protest against the British government's antifeminist policies.

Venus at Her Mirror, 1644-1648

Velázquez made his boldest experiment in technique when he painted *The Fable of Arachne (right)*, also known as *The Spinners*. The work was based on a classical myth. A Greek maiden, Arachne, boasted to her friends that she could spin and weave faster than Pallas Athena, the goddess of arts and crafts. Athena dressed herself as an old woman and, when Arachne repeated the boast to her, threw off the disguise and challenged the girl to a contest. Poor Arachne could not deliver on her claims; she lost, and was turned into a spider.

Using a loose, hazy style, Velázquez presents two episodes of the story. In the sunlit alcove Athena has tossed off her old woman's garb to stand before Arachne in breastplate and helmet. The foreground shows the contest between them in progress. Athena, at the left, appears again in her old woman's clothes, exposing a pleasant plump leg. Arachne, at right, winds her yarn as a girl delivers more wool to her. The frenzy of the contest is transmitted by Velázquez' innovations in the depiction of motion: the spokes of Athena's wheel are blurs, indicating the speed at which the goddess spins. Similarly, each of Arachne's fingers is depicted with several outlines; these convey a sense of busy fluttering as she winds her yarn *(detail, overleaf)*. The painting, now some five by eight feet in size, was enlarged—for reasons unknown—after Velázquez' death by the addition of painted strips to the top, sides and bottom, which appear slightly off-color.

The Fable of Arachne, 1644-1648

153

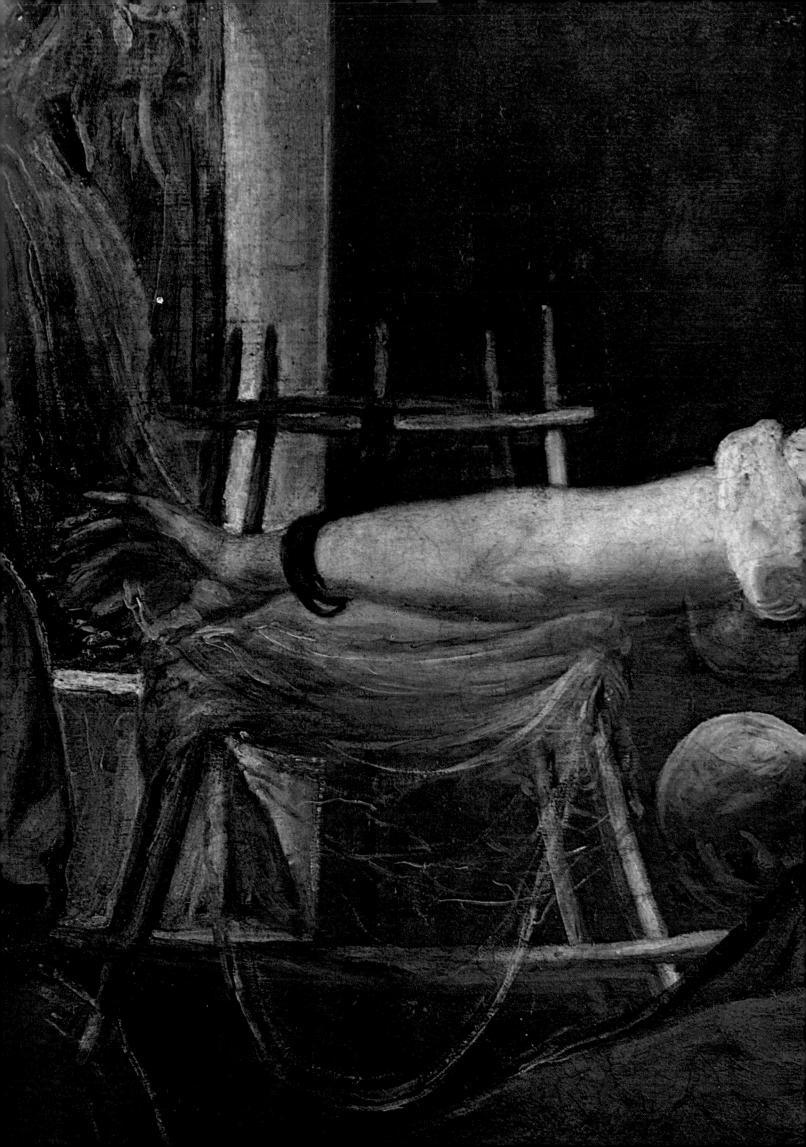

Villa Medici in Rome, date unknown

These two impressionistic sketches in oil of the Villa Medici in Rome are so modern in concept and execution that it is hard to believe they were painted in the 17th Century. In both works Velázquez manages a fleeting effect. He catches the interplay of shadow and sparkling sunlight, the rustling of the leaves in the breeze, the indolent saunter of the visitors in the gardens. Enhancing the transient nature of the moment, the brushstrokes are light and delicate, leaving the paint so thin that in many places it does not conceal the canvas beneath.

The scenes are unstaged, extremely casual—a novelty for a 17th Century artist. The villa and gardens could

Villa Medici in Rome, date unknown

have been treated with solemn deference, reminders of their splendid history. Once owned by members of the rich and powerful Medici family, the villa had housed a famous collection of classical sculpture. Velázquez, who lived there during his first Italian trip in 1630, manifestly admired his spacious surroundings, but at the same time took note of the pleasant irreverence with which the Italians treated their landmarks. In the painting above, a woman leans on what seems to be a bedsheet that she has draped over a marble balustrade and chats with two passersby. Beneath her, one of the villa's galleries is boarded over like the doorway of an abandoned store.

157

Pope Innocent X, 1650

erhaps Velázquez' greatest portrait, this incisive study of Innocent X *(detail, left)* was executed in Rome during the Jubilee Year of 1650, when the Eternal City was host to hordes of pilgrims, painters and sculptors from all over Europe. The painting caused a stir among them when it was unveiled, and no wonder. Innocent was a complex man—intelligent and kind, yet temperamental, suspicious and indecisive. He was a ruler of immense power, temporal as well as spiritual; moreover Velázquez hoped to gain his assistance in becoming a member of Spain's

religious-military order, the Knights of Santiago.

Nonetheless, all the elements of the man are there—the intelligence and the wariness emerge from Innocent's deep-set eyes, and there is decency writ upon the features as well. The hazily outlined, nervously moving fingers of the right hand contribute a sense of pent-up tension. To achieve his overall effect, Velázquez worked with successive layers of paint, building up, for example, the gleam of the red biretta, or cap, and short cape. The work, to everyone's surprise, pleased the Pope.

The Infanta Margarita, 1653

The Spanish court "wasted the fresh mornings in hunting for flowers, the days in feasts, and the nights in comedies," the contemporary diarist Barrionuevo wrote acidly. In this mindless milieu wandered Mariana of Austria, King Philip's niece and his second queen. At the time she posed for this Velázquez portrait *(opposite),* shortly after the artist's return from Italy, she was only 19 but had been Philip's wife for nearly five years. Her express function was to produce a sound male heir to the Spanish throne—a duty she failed to fulfill.

Mariana's costume holds her rigidly. But she seems not only physically but psychologically imprisoned, her plight revealed in her face *(detail, overleaf).* Under a plumed headdress of ribboned ringlets, the Queen's eyes reflect both petulance and melancholy.

A totally different quality pervades the artist's first portrait *(above)* of the Queen's daughter, the Princess Margarita, completed at about the same time. Bathed in soft, diffused light the chubby-cheeked Princess, then about two, radiates the innocence of childhood.

Queen Mariana, 1653

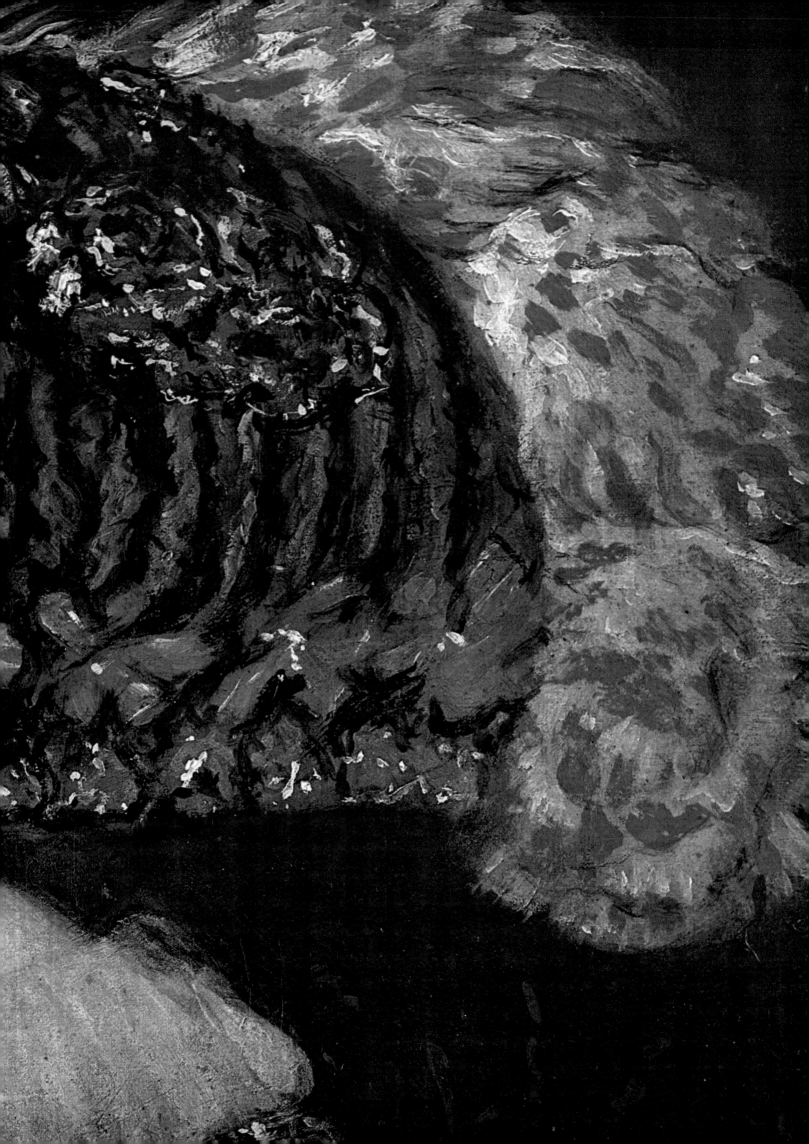

VII

An End to Glory

In the last decade of his life Velázquez gave fullest and freest expression to his personal style and produced the greatest of his paintings—one of the greatest of all paintings, *Las Meninas (The Ladies in Waiting)*. It is ironic and sad, then, that having come so far as an artist he should have let himself be distracted in these closing years by concerns other than art. And yet in this he was being true to himself. Until the end of his life, Velázquez remained a hidalgo, motivated by a desire for ever higher status.

Soon after he returned to Madrid from Italy in June 1651, he allowed his name to be put up for one of the most prestigious posts in the court hierarchy, that of Chamberlain to the King. The job was undeniably a plum. It paid handsomely—enough, certainly, to keep a gentleman in style —and it also provided a rent-free apartment in the Treasure House, next to the Alcázar. But along with its rewards it also had its responsibilities. The Chamberlain was in charge of the decoration of the royal palaces and the upkeep of their furnishings and art treasures. Moreover, he had to make all arrangements for the King's visits to the various royal residences, including, apparently, the laying in of supplies. This, in turn, required him to accompany the King on these jaunts to ensure that everything was carried out as planned.

To take on so heavy a work load and continue to paint at the same time was plainly difficult. Nevertheless, Velázquez seems to have actively sought the post, in competition with five other courtiers no less eager for advancement. For a time it appeared that his hopes were to be dashed; the official board set up to review the nominees' qualifications failed to put his name at the top of their list of recommended candidates from which the King was to make a choice. But Philip ignored the board's leading choices. In the margin of the report he tersely scribbled, "I name Velázquez," and that settled that. Velázquez became Chamberlain in March 1652.

Philip not only gratified his painter's ambition but also ordered that he be paid two years' back salary due him. That the King should proffer these tangible signs of his favor was in a sense surprising; he had been quite peevish over Velázquez' dallying in Italy. But these days he was in

The frail Prince Felipe Próspero, on whom rested all hopes for the continuation of the Habsburg line in Spain, is shown here, bedecked with charms to guard his health and protect him from evil. Velázquez painted this melancholy portrait when Felipe Próspero was two; the Prince died only two years later.

Prince Felipe Próspero, 1659

unusually fine fettle, court morale was improved, and the Buen Retiro was once more the scene of revelry. Even the theaters, shut down for seven years in a burst of piety, were open again.

Credit for the change of mood was due Spain's young and buxom new Queen, Mariana of Austria. Philip was entranced by her. She was self-willed and demanding, but vivacious as well. She loved gaiety and elicited it from those around her. On her honeymoon in the Escorial she had romped through the halls with her stepdaughter, María Teresa, who was only four years her junior; she also defied court etiquette by laughing out loud at the antics of Philip's dwarfs and buffoons. Philip poured out his happiness in a letter to the woman he trusted above all others, Sister María. "I confess to you," he wrote the nun, "that I do not know how I can thank our Lord for the favor He has shown me in giving me such a companion, for all the qualities I have seen up to the present in my niece are great, and I am extremely content."

There was only one thing wrong. Thus far the union of uncle and niece had failed in its main purpose—the procreation of a male heir. But at least Mariana's fertility was established. In July of 1652 she gave birth to a daughter, the Princess Margarita whom Velázquez was later to immortalize in *Las Meninas*, and there was no reason to believe that she would not soon produce a son.

In the ordinary course of events Velázquez would have painted the new Queen soon after her marriage; Philip's desire for a portrait of his adored bride may well have caused his annoyance over Velázquez' failure to hurry home from Italy. But by the time Velázquez got back to Madrid, the Queen was pregnant, and after her daughter's birth she lay ill for several months. The portrait had to be postponed, and instead Velázquez painted María Teresa, the only surviving child of Philip's first marriage. This was to be one of several portraits he and his assistants would execute of her in the next few years in response to requests from abroad; somewhat like photographs meant to display a model's charms, they were sent to foreign kings who wanted to "see" Philip's growingly eligible daughter. All that survives of Velázquez' portrait is the head. Because of the rouge smeared in large patches on María Teresa's cheeks, and the headdress she wears—an enormous arc of curls adorned with semicircular red bows—she looks much older than her 14 years.

The portrait is skillful enough, but there were better ones to follow. Despite the inroads that his duties as Chamberlain made on his time and energy, Velázquez was too much an artist to allow the quality of his painting to suffer, and the handful of works he produced in his eight remaining years ranks very high indeed. Among them were three brilliant portraits, each in its own way heralding his ultimate masterpiece, *Las Meninas*.

The first was a portrait of Queen Mariana at 19 *(page 161)*. When at last Velázquez tackled this project, he could not have found the task an easy one. His royal sitter seemed bent on showing her less attractive side. Fortunately for posterity, Velázquez made no attempt to disguise this fact in the portrait. Mariana stands erect in a tight bodice and an exaggeratedly wide hooped skirt. With her full Habsburg lips tightly pursed and her eyes fixed in a cold, imperious gaze, she looks very much the shrew. And yet what a superb portrait Velázquez produced. He devoted exquisite care to the rendering of Mariana's face, building it up from tissue-thin layers of paint *(detail, pages 162-163)*, and then, in contrast, he wielded his brush so loosely and freely in reproducing her dress and ornaments that their shimmering effects seem to have been achieved almost by sleight of hand.

If the Queen was a troublesome sitter, her daughter Margarita was plainly a more amenable one. By the looks of his four surviving portraits of the little Princess, Velázquez adored her. His paintings make her a live presence even today; charming and capricious, she still enchants viewers. His first portrait of Margarita dates from about 1653, when she was two *(page 160)*. It is the most delicately colored of all Velázquez' paintings. The Princess stands on a rug-covered dais in front of a blue-green drape, resting her tiny hand on a low table. Her plump face glows in a soft light, enclosed by an aureole of pale, blond hair. She wears a salmon-colored dress, trimmed with silver braid and black silk lace. There are pink bows on Margarita's wrists, at her waist and on her left shoulder, and these catch and reflect the light, as do her jewelry and the braid. The entire painting sparkles.

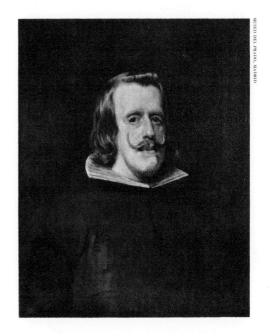

Velázquez' last portrait of Philip IV, painted at the depth of Spain's decline and only a few years before both artist and King died, reflects a powerful melancholy. As he had in every royal portrait since his first, Velázquez idealized the King's homely features. But the artist did not veil the sorrow—and perhaps even fear—that he saw in Philip's eyes. Posed against a somber background, the King is dressed as if in mourning, in a simple dark doublet and the *golilla* collar that he had inspired; indeed, at the time, Philip had ordered that no man be admitted to the royal presence unless he was dressed entirely in black.

In its wake, the portrait Velázquez painted of Philip at about the same time comes as a surprise. It is the most somber, the saddest, of the artist's works. Philip's face seems to have died: it just hangs there on the canvas, a mask from which pathetic eyes peer. By then life had lost all meaning for Philip. No male child had arrived to light up the future, and his marriage had turned sour; the Queen was incensed by his renewed philandering. (One caustic courtier commented in a letter that the King was a "fine hand at bastards," but had "very poor luck as regards legitimate children.")

The King's extramarital affairs, however, were more and more perfunctory. Though Philip was not yet 50, he behaved increasingly like an old man, finding little pleasure in the youthful games and festivities Mariana craved as the cure for her homesickness. In his letters to Sister María he spoke more often of her as his niece or as the Queen than as his wife, and sometimes he lumped her together with his daughters, referring to all three as "the girls." He was becoming a creature of habit; it was said that those who knew him well could predict what he would be doing on any given day a whole year in advance, so closely did he cling to a set routine. At public audiences he displayed no emotion, and when he spoke hardly a muscle in his face moved. On Friday mornings he would sit upon his throne and listen to secretaries read their reports; he would respond to their recommendations with only two words, *"Está bien"*—"It is well." When he received state papers from his Minister, Haro, he would generally sign and return them without comment, often without even reading them.

Undoubtedly Philip's financial situation contributed to his gloom. It was a shambles. In 1653 he again had to declare the Crown bankrupt —for the second time in six years. In 1654 he publicly admitted having an outstanding debt of 120 million ducats, without any hope of repaying it. He could count on little help from Spain's nobles, for they had been stripped of almost all their wealth in support of the never-ending war. The Church, too, had been drained, and the masses were ground down in abject poverty. Now more than ever cynicism permeated Spanish life. Murder and robbery were so common in Madrid that people hardly took notice. Prostitution flourished; out of a population of 250,000 to 300,000 Madrileños, about a tenth were women of easy virtue.

Philip's despair was magnified by his conviction that God detested him, and he sank into deep melancholy. In 1654 he viewed the remains of his ancestors and of his first wife, Isabel, which had been disinterred for reburial in the new mausoleum he had had built of gleaming marble and jasper at the Escorial *(page 134)*. He never got over what he saw. What disturbed him most was the sight of his great-grandfather's body. Although the corpse of Charles V had been in its coffin 96 years, it was almost perfectly preserved, and this Philip took as a sign of the great monarch's incorruptibility. He could only wonder how his own all-too-mortal flesh would fare. He began to return to the mausoleum to pray alone in front of the sarcophagus where one day he would lie. Once he spent as long as two hours kneeling on the hard floor, and when he emerged from the crypt someone noticed that the eyes of the normally emotionless King were red with weeping.

Looking again at Velázquez' portrait of him, it is almost possible to see the anxiety that immobilized Philip. He seems a man locked up, alone. One of the things that is so touching about this portrait is its sympathetic handling. No matter how much Philip may have blamed himself for Spain's miseries, Velázquez seems not to have blamed him at all. He painted him with all the feeling that he had poured into his pictures of those other afflicted, trapped and suffering souls, the court dwarfs.

This portrait may be the last Velázquez ever painted of Philip. A later, somewhat similar portrait in London's National Gallery has also been attributed to him, but many scholars have noted discrepancies in style between it and the earlier work and contend that it is either in part or entirely by Velázquez' son-in-law, Mazo. Thus the only other image of Philip that is unquestionably from Velázquez' hand in these waning years of Spain's greatness is found in *Las Meninas*. There, reflected in a smoky mirror on a gray-green wall in the background *(detail, page 184)*, are Philip and his queen, two wraithlike figures in a picture that otherwise is almost completely dominated by the shining presence of their five-year-old daughter Margarita.

When viewed against the dreary background of its time, *Las Meninas* would seem to have required an act of will on Velázquez' part to paint. Why would he have painted it at all? What led him to render on so grand a scale (the picture measures 10 by 9 feet) so casual a scene of court life—a moment in a day that must have been like all the days that preceded it and all that came after it? What rationale could he have had for bringing together in one picture himself, the Princess, two ladies in waiting, two dwarfs, a man and a woman in conversation, another man in a doorway and a dog—to say nothing of the King and Queen, reflected in the mirror?

Perhaps we need look no further than Velázquez' own private desires.

He was 56 years old. After more than three decades of royal service, he had reached the pinnacle of his career both as an artist and a courtier. And yet Velázquez still had one ambition, and that was to become a knight. He had already let Pope Innocent X know of his desire to enter one of the Spanish religious-military orders. What greater proof of his own worth, of his hidalgo's claim to nobility, could he have put forth at this particular time than *Las Meninas?*

Let us look at the painting *(page 178)*, and in particular, at Velázquez standing behind his wall of canvas—in effect, his shield. However modest a self-portrait this may be, there is no mistaking that he intended it to serve as a reminder of his achievements. He portrayed himself as a gentleman, wearing the insignia of his high office—the key of Chamberlain, seen as a faint glimmer at his waist. Moreover, he showed himself as part of the inner court circle, an intimate of the Royal Family; indeed, all the while he was painting *Las Meninas,* the King, Queen and the little Princess used to visit him and watch him at work. And as if showing himself in their company were not sign enough of the esteem in which he had come to be held by them, he went one step further and demonstrated how such regard gave him the freedom to paint as he pleased. Certainly he would never have been able to take so unorthodox a view of the Royal Family—in which a host of minor characters take precedence over the sovereigns who are seen only in the mirror—if he had not enjoyed the best of relationships with the King.

Yet whatever its practical motivations, *Las Meninas* is the noblest of all Velázquez' paintings, the culmination of his artistic growth. In *Las Meninas* he did more than record the facts of vision: he captured a living moment in a way no artist had ever done.

The fascination this painting held for the Royal Family is easy to imagine. They had never seen anything quite so real before, a man-made image that mirrored the world around them, down to the lamp hooks in the ceiling. Certainly they had cause to wonder, and their amazement must have been not unlike people's reactions to the first photographs. *Las Meninas* has much in common with a photograph—even with a snapshot. It is certainly a candid painting. All the poses are natural. All the expressions are valid. No one told the dwarfs to get out of the way; the stunted Mari-Bárbola, with her big head and wide-eyed stare, is one of the most memorable figures in the painting, a telling and touching foil to the little Princess.

The analogy with a photograph can be pursued further. As with a picture taken in a dimly lit room, only a portion of *Las Meninas* is in focus. Velázquez painted the dog a lot less precisely than the Princess, even though the dog lies in the foreground. Most other 17th Century artists would have rendered the animal in greater detail, laboring under the notion that the object closest to the eye is the one seen with greatest clarity. Velázquez knew otherwise; he knew because he let his eye be his guide—and his eye was focused on the Princess, not the dog. A photograph would have shown the same thing.

The British art critic, Sir Kenneth Clark, has written admiringly about *Las Meninas* in his collection of essays, *Looking at Pictures.* "It is not very difficult to paint a small inanimate object so that it seems real," Clark writes. "But when one begins to paint a figure in its setting 'Oh alors!' as Degas said. And to paint a whole group on a large scale in such a way that no one seems too prominent, each is related to the other, and all breathe the same air: that requires a most unusual gift." This gift Clark likens to perfect pitch.

Velázquez' perfect pitch manifested itself in his tonality. It is harmony of tone that makes the painting ring true in all its parts and makes each part relate to the whole. "Drawing may be summary, color drab," says Clark, "but if the relations of tone are true, the picture will hold." *Las Meninas* holds.

One of the amazing—and haunting—aspects of *Las Meninas* is its point of view. It was meant to be seen from roughly the same spot where the King and Queen would have had to stand in order to be reflected in the mirror. In a sense, we see the scene through their eyes: we are with them in Velázquez' studio, an illusion made all the more real by the picture's lifelike dimensions. But no painting is ever viewed from one angle, and *Las Meninas* can be approached from many angles and appreciated from up close as well as from a distance. Then one sees that this is the most broadly painted of Velázquez' works, accented with sharp strokes of the brush, glorifying the paint itself *(detail, page 179)*. Remarking on the changing aspects of *Las Meninas*, Sir Kenneth tells how he used to stalk the picture: "I would start from as far away as I could, when the illusion was complete, and come gradually nearer, until suddenly what had been a hand, and a ribbon, and a piece of velvet, dissolved into a salad of beautiful brush strokes. I thought I might learn something if I could catch the moment at which this transformation took place, but it proved to be as elusive as the moment between waking and sleeping."

After completing *Las Meninas*, Velázquez undoubtedly felt let down. He had put as much of himself into it as he had into any of his pictures —probably a great deal more. Yet in a way this extraordinary portrayal of court life may have seemed to him an exercise in futility. Everywhere around him there was gloom and decay, enough to drain even the strongest-willed of men of their energies. The path of Spain was increasingly downhill.

In 1656 a second daughter was born to Philip and Mariana, and died soon after birth. The Queen became depressed and Philip more listless than ever. Not only deprived of a son, they were also deprived of the money that would have allowed them diversions to drown their sorrow. Poverty had swept right into the palace, and Philip, who should have been Europe's richest monarch, was now its poorest. Not one ducat from the colonies had reached Madrid for a couple of years; the once-friendly English had turned against Spain and were seizing the ships of the Silver Fleet on the high seas. The King was so impoverished that by 1657 the shopkeepers of Madrid were refusing him credit. "For the last two months and a half," a courtier confessed in a letter, "the usual rations have not been distributed in the palace, for the King has not a real. On the day of St. Francis they served a capon to the Princess María Teresa who ordered them to take it away, as it stank like a dead dog. They then brought her a chicken, of which she is very fond, on sippets of toast, but it was so covered with flies that she nearly overturned the lot. This is how things go in the palace."

But just when things were at their worst, a miracle happened—or so it seemed. A male heir to the throne was born. He was baptized Felipe Próspero, and the greatest care was taken to ensure his survival. Philip had had his share of disappointments, but the thought of losing another son was more than he could bear. He wrote movingly to Sister María, asking once again for her prayers: "Pray to our Lord and His Holy Mother to keep him for their service, for the exaltation of the faith and the good of these realms. If this is not to be, then pray let him be taken from me before he reaches manhood."

Felipe Próspero was a pale, sickly child—an epileptic. When Velázquez painted his sad portrait at the age of two *(page 164),* he showed him adorned with assorted charms. The red rosette and the black amulet in the shape of a hand on the prince's left shoulder were meant to ward off the evil eye; the pomander ball attached to the gold chain on his chest to guard against disease; and the silver bell dangling from his waist to protect him from witchcraft. Feeble as he was, Felipe Próspero managed to survive from year to year, and however anxious these years may have been for his doting parents, they did make it seem as though there might be a future for the monarchy.

For Velázquez, who lived so close to the Royal Family and the dying

Velázquez' chief joys in his old age were his grandchildren, the offspring of his daughter Francisca and his artist son-in-law Martínez del Mazo, who painted this family portrait. At the time the picture was painted Francisca had died and Mazo had married the seated woman and begun a second family. Velázquez continued to aid his son-in-law's career after the loss of his daughter and to provide, both directly and indirectly, for the welfare of his grandchildren. Gaspar, the eldest boy, was given the position at court of Usher to the Chamber, a sinecure that Velázquez himself had held and had passed on to Mazo as a dowry for Francisca. Mazo's fifth child had as his godfather Prince Baltasar Carlos. As far as is known, none of the children carried on the family tradition by becoming artists. Mazo—who depicted himself at an easel in the right background —is known as an artist chiefly because of his relationship with Velázquez.

power of Spain, this must have been an especially bleak time, but it was not an unrewarding one. He completed the decoration of the Alcázar and also produced four pictures on mythological themes for a new room called the Hall of Mirrors. Of these, only one survives—*Mercury and Argus,* a long, narrow panel showing a brooding, dimly lit scene in which Mercury sneaks up on the sleeping Argus to deal him a deathblow. Velázquez also painted three royal portraits—that of little Felipe Próspero, another of Princess Margarita and a miniature of the Queen. These were his last works.

In 1658 he saw within reach the honor he had so long desired: the King proposed that Velázquez be made a knight as the reward for his long and loyal service, and that he be allowed to join the Order of Santiago, to which only noblemen were admitted. But before he could become a member, he had first to show that he descended from a noble line of ancestors and that he had neither Jewish nor Moorish blood. He had also to demonstrate that he had lived his life as a gentleman, and had never painted for a living. Some 140 people were willing to come forward and testify for him, and a few were anxious enough to see him become a knight to stretch the truth on his behalf. These loyal supporters —including the painter Zurbarán—were happy to assert that Velázquez had never had a master, never had a workshop and had never sold any of his pictures. As they described him, he was a man who painted only for his own pleasure and that of the King.

Establishing Velázquez' noble ancestry was not so easy. Investigations conducted in Madrid, Seville and areas close to Portugal where his family had lived were inconclusive. This might have been a real stumbling block to his investiture had not Philip seen a way to cut through all the red tape. He wrote to his Ambassador in Rome and asked him to take up the matter with Pope Alexander VII, Innocent's successor. The Pope's response was quick and in the affirmative; the requirement of noble birth was waived, and on November 28, 1659, Diego de Silva Velázquez became a knight of the Order of Santiago. Soon thereafter the emblem of the Order was added to his costume in *Las Meninas,* perhaps by Velázquez himself, although legend has it that it was the King who painted it on the canvas.

Velázquez' life was drawing to a close. Although he had fulfilled the promise of his youth, he had seen all of Spain's dreams die. The country lay utterly exhausted. The years of national sacrifice had come to nothing. Though Catalonia had finally grown weary of the French and thrown in its lot once again with Castile, Portugal remained outside the fold, never to return. In Flanders the French were pounding away at Spanish defenses, and city after city fell to them. But they, too, were having their political troubles at home, and it must have been as apparent to them as it was to the Spaniards that the war had gone on far too long. Besides, now that Spain stood revealed as a hollow giant, what was there to fear from her?

Negotiations got underway between the French and Spaniards in August 1659, and led to a truce the following May. Considering that France had the upper hand, it is surprising how lightly Spain got off when the

Sealing the marriage contract with a bow and a handshake, Philip IV hands his daughter, María Teresa, over to young King Louis XIV of France in this tableau from a 17th Century tapestry designed by Charles Le Brun. Louis was Philip's nephew but it was hoped that this further union would bring peace between the two Catholic powers. With her bad French, unfashionable trousseau and childlike enthusiasm for dwarfs and puppies, María Teresa cut less than an elegant figure at Versailles. But she was a loyal queen, and of her death Louis gallantly remarked, "This is the only annoyance she has ever caused me."

peace treaty was signed. She had to relinquish some Catalonian territory that had formerly been French and give up her hold on part of Flanders, but essentially her territorial possessions remained as they had been before the war started. The peace thus obtained was to be perpetuated through the marriage of Philip's daughter María Teresa and the young French king, Louis XIV. Philip could agree to this without fear that it might result in a union of France and Spain after his death, because he now had a son who presumably one day would marry and carry on the Habsburg line.

It fell to Velázquez, as Chamberlain, to make many of the arrangements for the wedding. A difficult assignment under the best of circumstances, it was complicated by the fact that the ceremonies were to take place not in Madrid, but in three places some 250 miles to the north: in the Spanish town of Fuenterrabía; on the Isle of Pheasants, which straddles the Spanish-French border; and in the French village of Saint-Jean-de-Luz. Velázquez left Madrid on April 8, 1660, two weeks ahead of the King. Part of his task was to inspect and reserve lodgings along the way for the royal party. He traveled in a litter, accompanied by several assistants riding mules. One of his helpers was a carpenter whose duty it was to secure members of the royal party against robbers by fixing the doors and locks of the buildings in which they were to stay. The journey north took 24 days. At the end of it Velázquez presumably turned his attention to the important business of decorating the Spanish section of the pavilion on the Isle of Pheasants where the bride was to be handed over to her groom.

In the meantime, the royal party had started out from Madrid in a caravan that stretched 20 miles along the road and progressed at the rate of six miles a day. A last great effort had been made to create an impression of vast wealth. The King took his costliest jewels with him and transported his household in 14 coaches drawn by six mules apiece. His Minister, Haro, brought along 200 attendants. Folded away in trunks were the magnificent clothes with which the Spaniards hoped to stir the envy of the French.

After six weeks en route, the royal party arrived at Fuenterrabía. A day or so later a weeping María Teresa was married by proxy to Louis XIV in a Spanish ceremony at Fuenterrabía, with Haro standing in for the 22-year-old French king. Then the bride and her father proceeded to the Isle of Pheasants, and Velázquez was accorded the honor of going with them. He wore a rich costume, trimmed with silver lace, and sported a small ceremonial sword at his side. On his cape was stitched the red cross of the Order of Santiago, and dangling from a gold chain around his neck was a diamond-studded medallion, enameled with the emblem of the order of knighthood. Thus it was as a nobleman —and not simply as painter to the King—that he witnessed the historic moment when Philip gave his daughter, "this piece of my own heart," to Louis XIV. In that one moment the two monarchs stood face to face: Philip, who had been known as the Planet King, was a worn-out old man; Louis, *Le Roi Soleil,* the Sun King, had youth and vigor, and the whole future stretched ahead of him. It must have been sadly apparent to Velázquez, so accustomed to seeing the truth, that France's sun was now in the ascendancy.

Philip's courtiers had come to the wedding to dazzle the French with their brilliance, and they found themselves dazzled by the French instead. The new fashions of Paris made those of Madrid seem hopelessly old-fashioned. Shoulder-length periwigs and red high heels were just two of the innovations in men's wear that caused envious comment among the Spaniards. Their reaction is conveyed by a passage in one of the newsletters of the day: "Many of our courtiers write that the French gentlemen and ladies who came to the ceremonies were so numerous, and the adornments they wore were so rich and abundant, that we were evidently inferior to them, although much care had been taken on our side to excel, and no expense had been spared. So we cannot say this time, as we have said before, that the French finery was nothing but frills, furbelows, and feathers."

Velázquez returned to Madrid in the royal entourage. Soon afterward he wrote to a painter friend in Valladolid. The letter is one of the very few we have in Velázquez' own handwriting and in his own words. In it he reveals himself a man of gentle temperament: "Dear Sir, I shall be very happy if this finds you in the good health which I desire for you and also for my lady Doña María. I, Sir, arrived at this court Saturday at dawn on June twenty-sixth, weary of traveling by night and working by day, but in good health, and thanks to God, I found my household in the same condition. His Majesty arrived the same day and the Queen went out to meet him. . . . The Queen is very pretty, and so is the Prince, our master; last Wednesday there was a bullfight in the Plaza Mayor but without horsemen, so that it was a simple affair. . . . Please give me news of your health, Sir, and that of my lady, Doña María, and command me in what way I may serve you, because I am always very much at your orders. To our friend, Tomás de Peñas, give many regards from me because I was so busy and came away in such a hurry that I could not see him; there is nothing here to tell you about, only that God keep you for me many years, as I desire."

Velázquez was 61 years old; despite what he said in his letter about being well, his health seems to have deteriorated. Before his return a rumor had reached Madrid that he was dead. The journey and his duties had put a heavy strain on him; and on the last day of July 1660, while he was attending the King, he complained of feeling feverish and tired. He asked to be excused and went to his quarters in the Treasure House. There he began to experience severe pains in his heart and stomach. A doctor was called who diagnosed his illness as tertian fever—malaria. The King quickly sent the Patriarch of the Indies, an important prelate of the Church, to give the painter spiritual comfort. On August 6, after naming an executor, Velázquez received the Last Sacrament, and that afternoon died; he was to be followed to the grave one week later by Juana, his wife of 43 years. Clad in the robes of the Order of Santiago, his body was laid out in his bedroom, and buried the next night in the Church of San Juan Bautista. Attending the burial were many nobles and servants. Some time later, when the King, whom Velázquez had assured immortality, was asked to approve a settlement of the painter's salary, he is supposed to have scrawled on the document, "I am overcome."

Velázquez died just in time. Had he lived longer, he would have seen Philip's reign draw to a mournful close. The Prince of so many hopes and prayers, the frail Felipe Próspero, died in his fourth year, on November 1, 1661. A few days later another male child was born to the King and Queen, and though his birth caused much rejoicing, the awful truth was soon undeniable: little Carlos was grotesquely twisted in body and feeble in mind.

Philip staggered on. After the death of his Minister, Haro, he tried once again to rule on his own, and once again he attempted a cleanup of Madrid's crime and corruption. "I am quite old enough now to see things for myself," he declared, "and I shall be glad if those who know of anything that needs remedying will advise me of it, and I will see to it." But it was too late. Retribution for his sins seemed to pour down on him. His efforts to recover Portugal failed, and just before defeat in a final campaign in 1665, he learned that Sister María, the voice of his conscience, had died. Now Philip was completely alone, and it was more than he could bear. At the news that the Portuguese had slashed his army from 15,000 men to 8,000 in eight hours, he threw himself upon the floor and sobbed "Oh, God! Thy will be done." It was the first time anyone had seen the King break down.

Philip lived out his last days in fear of eternal damnation, wracked by fevers and pierced by the pain of gallstones. Some said that he had fallen under a witch's spell, and preparations were made to drive the evil spirit from him. But Philip, and everyone else, must have known the end was near. On his deathbed he said to his four-year-old heir, Carlos, "God make you happier than he has made me." He died on September 17, 1665. A courtier noted that in the palace only three people wept at his passing "and in all the rest of the capital there was not one person who shed a tear."

Philip IV's son and successor on the throne of Spain was Carlos II, a scrofulous, ricket-ridden, ulcerated testimony to the perils of the Habsburgs' habitual inbreeding. As the years passed, his hair fell out, his teeth rotted, his bones weakened, his eyesight dimmed, and he was stricken with paralytic distemper. As a final curse—or perhaps it was a blessing for Spain—he was impotent. This misbegotten monarch, known to his subjects as Carlos the Bewitched, died in 1700 at the age of 39. The portrait is the work of the Spanish painter Claudio Coello.

Velázquez executed his finest work, *Las Meninas* *(overleaf, and on the following pages)*, in the waning days of Spain's glory. All around him he saw gloom, and yet glowing at the center of this informal scene of palace life is a ray of hope—the five-year-old Princess Margarita, daughter of Philip IV by his second marriage, to his niece and cousin, Mariana of Austria.

Never did Velázquez express himself more fully—or more boldly—than in *Las Meninas*, utilizing the broad expanse of his 10-by-9-foot canvas to sum up his art. He even portrayed himself in it *(right)*, at work on a large painting that may be *Las Meninas* itself. Standing behind this canvas, he is the observer as well as the creator of the perfectly composed scene—and what he has painted is not just the group of figures and the dim room in which they stand, but the space around them and the soft light that defines them. Marveling over Velázquez' accomplishment, the 17th Century Italian artist Luca Giordano hailed the picture as "the theology of Painting." After seeing *Las Meninas* and other works by Velázquez, Édouard Manet, the first of the great modern artists, called Velázquez "the painter's painter." But for all its technical brilliance—and in spite of the radiant Margarita—there is something melancholy about this masterpiece, as though Velázquez, who had always concerned himself with the truth, intended it as a *memento mori,* a reminder that all things pass, even little princesses.

"Las Meninas": The Theology of Painting

The self-portrait in *Las Meninas* reveals Velázquez' pride in the accomplishments—and emblems —of his courtier's career. His sensitive hands hold brush and palette, the Palace Chamberlain's key hangs at his belt, and the red cross of the Knights of Santiago decorates his somber doublet.

Detail from *Las Meninas*

Las Meninas, 1656

178

Detail, *Las Meninas*, 1656

Everything about *Las Meninas* is real. All but one of the people in it are known by name; the two at right are the dwarfs Mari-Bárbola and Nicolas Pertusato. The canvases on the walls are replicas of Flemish works by the artist's son-in-law, Mazo. The room, Velázquez' studio in the Alcázar, was once part of the quarters occupied by Baltasar Carlos before his death at 17. In the mirror can be seen a reflection of the King and Queen, looking in at the scene. Viewed up close, as in the detail above, which is reproduced actual size, and in the details on the following pages, the precise imagery of *Las Meninas* seems to melt—and another reality takes over. It is the artist's brushwork, quick, assured, the mark of a man fully aware of his powers, but disinclined to show them off.

Velázquez blurred the Habsburg features of King Philip IV and his wife when he painted their double portrait as a mirror reflection. What we see are the mere shadows of majesty. It is as though Velázquez had in mind a line about the court written by the poet Quevedo: "There are many things here that seem to exist and have their being, and yet they are nothing more than a name and an appearance." The tide of Spanish power, apparently supreme on three continents at the beginning of Philip's reign, was fast ebbing. Portugal was lost, and with it Brazil; other overseas lands were threatened by the Protestant Dutch and English, who plundered the Silver Fleets that propped Spain's tottering economy. Less than 10 years after *Las Meninas* was painted, the King died, leaving a half-witted four-year-old heir to the Crown. The boy, Carlos II, was the last of the Habsburg line in Spain. His sister, the golden-haired Margarita, fared hardly better; although she became empress of Austria at 15, she died at 22. But, thanks to her father's painter, her youth and beauty survived her, in *Las Meninas.*

Chronology: Artists of Velázquez' Era

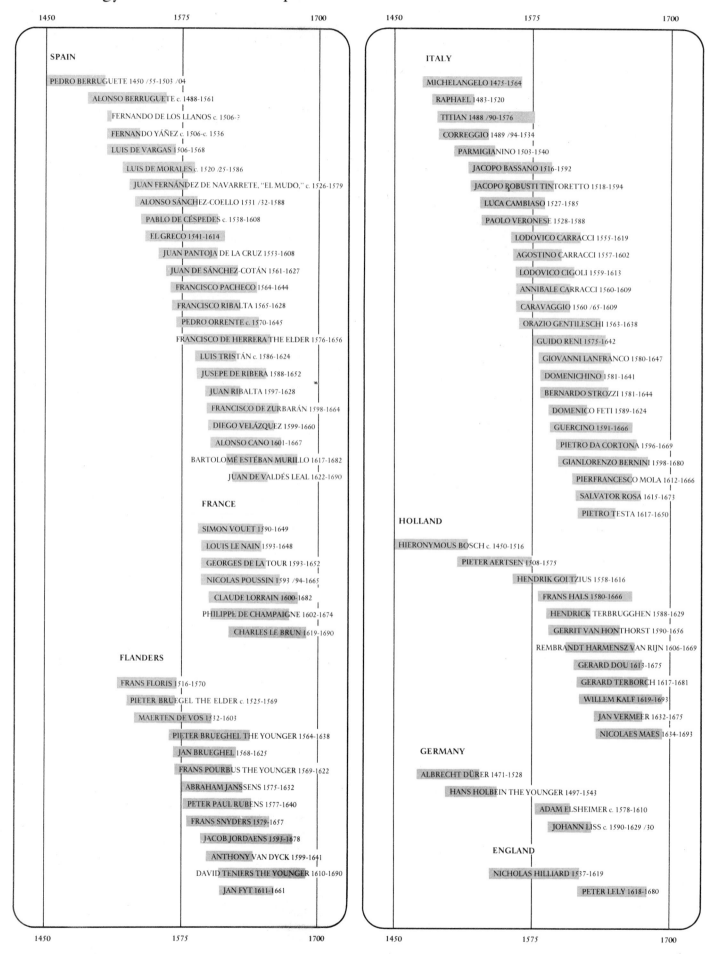

SPAIN	
PEDRO BERRUGUETE 1450 /55-1503 /04	
ALONSO BERRUGUETE c. 1488-1561	
FERNANDO DE LOS LLANOS c. 1506-?	
FERNANDO YÁÑEZ c. 1506-c. 1536	
LUIS DE VARGAS 1506-1568	
LUIS DE MORALES c. 1520 /25-1586	
JUAN FERNÁNDEZ DE NAVARRETE, "EL MUDO," c. 1526-1579	
ALONSO SÁNCHEZ-COELLO 1531 /32-1588	
PABLO DE CÉSPEDES c. 1538-1608	
EL GRECO 1541-1614	
JUAN PANTOJA DE LA CRUZ 1553-1608	
JUAN DE SÁNCHEZ-COTÁN 1561-1627	
FRANCISCO PACHECO 1564-1644	
FRANCISCO RIBALTA 1565-1628	
PEDRO ORRENTE c. 1570-1645	
FRANCISCO DE HERRERA THE ELDER 1576-1656	
LUIS TRISTÁN c. 1586-1624	
JUSEPE DE RIBERA 1588-1652	
JUAN RIBALTA 1597-1628	
FRANCISCO DE ZURBARÁN 1598-1664	
DIEGO VELÁZQUEZ 1599-1660	
ALONSO CANO 1601-1667	
BARTOLOMÉ ESTÉBAN MURILLO 1617-1682	
JUAN DE VALDÉS LEAL 1622-1690	

FRANCE

SIMON VOUET 1590-1649
LOUIS LE NAIN 1593-1648
GEORGES DE LA TOUR 1593-1652
NICOLAS POUSSIN 1593 /94-1665
CLAUDE LORRAIN 1600-1682
PHILIPPE DE CHAMPAIGNE 1602-1674
CHARLES LE BRUN 1619-1690

FLANDERS

FRANS FLORIS 1516-1570
PIETER BRUEGEL THE ELDER c. 1525-1569
MAERTEN DE VOS 1532-1603
PIETER BRUEGHEL THE YOUNGER 1564-1638
JAN BRUEGHEL 1568-1625
FRANS POURBUS THE YOUNGER 1569-1622
ABRAHAM JANSSENS 1575-1632
PETER PAUL RUBENS 1577-1640
FRANS SNYDERS 1579-1657
JACOB JORDAENS 1593-1678
ANTHONY VAN DYCK 1599-1641
DAVID TENIERS THE YOUNGER 1610-1690
JAN FYT 1611-1661

ITALY

MICHELANGELO 1475-1564
RAPHAEL 1483-1520
TITIAN 1488 /90-1576
CORREGGIO 1489 /94-1534
PARMIGIANINO 1503-1540
JACOPO BASSANO 1516-1592
JACOPO ROBUSTI TINTORETTO 1518-1594
LUCA CAMBIASO 1527-1585
PAOLO VERONESE 1528-1588
LODOVICO CARRACCI 1555-1619
AGOSTINO CARRACCI 1557-1602
LODOVICO CIGOLI 1559-1613
ANNIBALE CARRACCI 1560-1609
CARAVAGGIO 1560 /65-1609
ORAZIO GENTILESCHI 1563-1638
GUIDO RENI 1575-1642
GIOVANNI LANFRANCO 1580-1647
DOMENICHINO 1581-1641
BERNARDO STROZZI 1581-1644
DOMENICO FETI 1589-1624
GUERCINO 1591-1666
PIETRO DA CORTONA 1596-1669
GIANLORENZO BERNINI 1598-1680
PIERFRANCESCO MOLA 1612-1666
SALVATOR ROSA 1615-1673
PIETRO TESTA 1617-1650

HOLLAND

HIERONYMOUS BOSCH c. 1450-1516
PIETER AERTSEN 1508-1575
HENDRIK GOLTZIUS 1558-1616
FRANS HALS 1580-1666
HENDRICK TERBRUGGHEN 1588-1629
GERRIT VAN HONTHORST 1590-1656
REMBRANDT HARMENSZ VAN RIJN 1606-1669
GERARD DOU 1613-1675
GERARD TERBORCH 1617-1681
WILLEM KALF 1619-1693
JAN VERMEER 1632-1675
NICOLAES MAES 1634-1693

GERMANY

ALBRECHT DÜRER 1471-1528
HANS HOLBEIN THE YOUNGER 1497-1543
ADAM ELSHEIMER c. 1578-1610
JOHANN LISS c. 1590-1629 /30

ENGLAND

NICHOLAS HILLIARD 1537-1619
PETER LELY 1618-1680

Velázquez' predecessors, contemporaries and successors are grouped chronologically by country. The bands correspond to the artists' life spans.

Bibliography *Available in paperback

CULTURAL AND HISTORICAL BACKGROUND

The Book of Saints. Compiled by the Benedictine Monks of St. Augustine's Abbey, Ramsgate. 5th ed. Thomas Y. Crowell, 1966.

Calvert, Albert F. (editor), *The Escorial.* The Spanish Series. The Bodley Head, London.

Chapman, Charles E., *A History of Spain.** The Free Press, 1965.

Cirici-Pellicer, Alejandro, *Treasures of Spain.* Albert Skira, Geneva, 1965.

Clark, Kenneth, *Looking at Pictures.* Holt, Rinehart & Winston, 1960.

Davies, R. Trevor, *The Golden Century of Spain, 1501-1621.* Macmillan, London, 1954.

Elliott, J. H.:
"The Decline of Spain" in *Crisis in Europe.** Anchor Books, 1967.
*Imperial Spain, 1469-1716.** Mentor Books, 1966.
The Revolt of the Catalans. Cambridge University Press, 1963.

Ferguson, George, *Signs and Symbols in Christian Art.* Oxford University Press, 1954.

Hendy, Philip, *Spanish Painting.* Avalon Press, London, 1946.

Hughes, Philip:
A History of the Church. Vol. 3. Sheed and Ward, 1947.
A Popular History of the Catholic Church. Macmillan, 1947.

Hume, Martin, *The Court of Philip IV.* Eveleigh House, London, 1907.

Jedlicka, Gotthard, *Spanish Painting.* Viking Press, 1963.

Kendrick, T. D., *Mary of Ágreda: The Life and Legend of a Spanish Nun.* Routledge and Kegan Paul, London, 1967.

Kubler, George, and Martin Soria, *Art and Architecture in Spain and Portugal and Their American Dominions, 1500-1800.* Penguin Books, Baltimore, 1959.

Lassaigne, Jacques, *Spanish Painting from the Catalan Frescoes to El Greco.* Translated by Stuart Gilbert. Albert Skira, Geneva, 1952.

López-Serrano, Matilde, *El Escorial.* Madrid, 1966.

McGuigan, Dorothy Gies, *The Habsburgs.* Doubleday, 1966.

Magurn, Ruth S. (editor), *The Letters of Peter Paul Rubens.* Harvard University Press, 1955.

Mâle, Émil, *Religious Art from the Twelfth to the Eighteenth Century.** The Noonday Press, 1949.

Moreno Villa, José, *Locos, Enanos, Negros y Niños Palaciegos.* La Casa de España en México, 1939.

Smith, Bradley, *Spain, A History in Art.* Simon and Schuster, 1966.

Tapié, Victor L., *The Age of Grandeur.* Grove Press, 1957.

Trevor-Roper, Hugh (editor), *The Age of Expansion.* McGraw-Hill, 1968.

Wedgwood, C. V., *The Thirty Years War.* Jonathan Cape, Ltd., London, 1939.

Wemble, Harry B., *Great Paintings from the Prado.* Harry N. Abrams, 1963.

VELÁZQUEZ—HIS LIFE AND WORK

Beruete, Aureliano de, *Velázquez.* Methuen and Company, London, 1906.

Justi, Karl, *Diego Velázquez und sein jahrhundert.* Bonn, 1933.

Lafuente, Enrique, *Velázquez.* Phaidon Press, London, 1943.

López-Rey, José:
Velázquez: A Catalogue Raisonné of His Oeuvre. Faber and Faber, London, 1963.
Velázquez' Work and World. Faber and Faber, London, 1968.

Ortega y Gasset, José, *Velázquez.* New York, 1953.

Riggs, Arthur Stanley, *Velázquez: Painter of Truth and Prisoner of the King.* Bobbs-Merrill, 1947.

Stevenson, R. A. M., *Velázquez.* C. Bell and Sons, Ltd., London, 1962.

Trapier, Elizabeth du Gué, *Velázquez.* The Hispanic Society of America, 1948.

Varia Velazqueña, 2 vols. Ministerio de Educación Nacional, Madrid, 1960.

ON OTHER ARTISTS

Braham, Allan, *Murillo.** Purnell & Sons, Ltd., Paulton, 1966.

Cargol, Joaquin Pla, *Ribera y Zurbarán.* Dalmu Carles, Madrid, 1944.

Curtis, Charles B., *A Description and Historical Catalogue of the Works of Velázquez and Murillo.* J. W. Bouton, 1883.

Guinard, Paul, *El Greco.* Albert Skira, Lausanne, 1956.

Kelemen, Pál, *El Greco Revisited: Candia-Venice-Toledo.* Macmillan, 1961.

Keysor, Jennie Ellis, *Murillo and Spanish Art.* Educational Publishing, 1899.

Legendre, M., and A. Hartman, *Domenikos Theotokopoulos Called El Greco.* Commodore Press, London, 1937.

Scott, William B., *Murillo and the Spanish School of Painting.* G. Routledge, London, 1873.

Soria, Martin S., *The Paintings of Zurbarán.* Phaidon Publishers, Garden City Books, 1953.

Trapier, Elizabeth du Gué, *Ribera.* The Hispanic Society of America, 1952.

Venturi, Lionello, *From Leonardo to El Greco.* Albert Skira, Geneva, 1956.

Wethey, Harold E., *El Greco and His School,* 2 vols. Princeton University Press, 1962.

Picture Credits

The sources for the illustrations in this book appear below. Credits for pictures from left to right are separated by semicolons, from top to bottom by dashes.

SLIPCASE: Manso.

END PAPERS:
Front: Guido Sansoni.
Back: Guido Sansoni.

CHAPTER 1: 6—Manso. 9—Oesterreichische Nationalbibliothek, Vienna. 13 —Manso. 14—Manso; Meadows Museum at Southern Methodist University, Dallas. 15—Alinari; National Gallery, London. 16—© Peter C. Scheier; Courtesy of The Hispanic Society of America, New York. 20—The American Numismatic Society, New York. 25—The National Maritime Museum, Greenwich, England. 26, 27—Kunsthistorisches Museum, Vienna (2) —Guido Sansoni. 28, 29—©Rijksmuseum, Amsterdam. 30, 31—Manso. CHAPTER 2: 32—Manso. 34—Det Kongelige Bibliotek, Copenhagen. 35 —Foto Mas. 36—Biblioteca Riccardiana, Florence. 42—Foto Mas. 43 —John R. Freeman. 45—Tom Scott, courtesy National Gallery of Scotland, Edinburgh. 46, 47—Derek Bayes. 48 through 51—National Gallery, London. 52, 53—Manso. 54, 55—Derek Bayes. CHAPTER 3: 56—Ivan Massar from Black Star. 58—National Gallery, London. 60—Bibliothèque Nationale, Paris. 62—Courtesy The Hispanic Society of America, New York. 64—Lee Boltin—Parke-Bernet Galleries Inc., New

York. 65—© A.C.L. Bruxelles. 69-71—Manso. 72, 73—Scala. 74-78—Manso. 79—Lee Boltin. 80-83—Manso. CHAPTER 4: 84—Lee Boltin. 87—Foto Mas. 91—Graphische Sammlung Albertina, Vienna. 93, 94—Foto Mas. 95, 96, 97—Manso. 98—Wadsworth Atheneum, Hartford, Conn. 99—Lee Boltin. 100, 101—Manso; Editorial Photocolor Archives, Inc. 102, 103—Manso. CHAPTER 5: 104—© The Frick Collection, New York. 108—Bibliothèque Nationale, Paris. 110—Print Division, New York Public Library. 112, 113 —Anderson-Giraudon. 115—Wellington Museum, London. 121—Anderson-Giraudon. 122, 123—Manso. 124—Giraudon; Manso. 125— Foto Mas; Staatliche Kunstsammlungen, Kassel. 126—Foto Mas. 127— Anderson-Giraudon. 128, 129—Anderson. 130—Foto Mas. 131—Anderson. 132—Anderson-Giraudon. 133—Foto Mas. CHAPTER 6: 134—Evelyn Hofer. 137—Bancroft Library, University of California, Berkeley. 138, 139—Lee Boltin. 143—Foto Mas. 146—Alinari. 147 —Vatican Medal Collection. 149—Derek Bayes. 150, 151—National Gallery, London. 152 through 155—Manso. 156, 157—Lee Boltin. 158 —Marzari. 159—Scala. 160—Erich Lessing from Magnum. 161, 162, 163—Manso. CHAPTER 7: 164—Erich Lessing from Magnum. 167—Manso. 171—Kunsthistorisches Museum, Vienna. 173—Dmitri Kessel. 175 through 184— Manso.

Acknowledgments

The author and editors of this book particularly wish to thank José López-Rey, whose books were essential sources of information for this volume. They also wish to thank the following persons and institutions: José Camón Aznar, Director, Museo Lázaro Galdeano, Madrid; Berta Maracchi Biagiarelli, Biblioteca Medicea-Laurenziana, Florence; Francisco Javier Sánchez Cantón, Director, Real Academia de Bellas Artes de San Fernando, Madrid; Xavier De Salas, Assistant Director, Museo del Prado, Madrid; Leslie A. Elam, Editor, The American Numismatic Society, New York; Italo Faldi, Galleria Doria-Pamphilj, Rome; Gabinetto Nazionale delle Stampe, Rome; Henry Grunthal, Curator of European and Modern Coins, The American Numismatic Society, New York; the Staff of The Hispanic Society of America, New York; Diego Angulo Iñiguez, Director, Museo del Prado, Madrid; Cécile de Jandin, Bibliothécaire Cabinet des Estampes, Bibliothèque Nationale, Paris; Dr. Walter Koschatzky, Director, Graphische Sammlung Albertina, Vienna; Frans Maes, Director, Belgian Information Service, New York; Antonietta Morandini, Biblioteca Riccardiana, Florence; The National Gallery, London; Helen Pernice, Print Room, Cincinnati Art Museum; Charles F. Stevens, Director of Public Relations, United States Playing Card Company, Cincinnati; Luigi Michelini Tocci, Medal Collection, Vatican Library, Rome; Irma Merolle Tondi, Biblioteca Riccardiana, Florence; Victor Velen, Florence; and the Wellington Museum, London.

Index

Numerals in italics indicate a picture of the subject mentioned. Unless otherwise specified, all listed art works are by Velázquez. Dimensions are given in inches; height precedes width.

189

Index (continued)

The typeface employed in this book is called Janson, after Anton Janson, the Dutch typefounder who popularized it in Leipzig in the late 17th Century. The face was first cut, however, by Nicholas Kis, a Hungarian working in Amsterdam in the 1680s.

xxx

PRINTED IN U.S.A.